THE PROBABILITY OF ADDICTION

LEGAL, MEDICAL AND SOCIAL IMPLICATIONS

D1269520

DAVID A. PETERS

THE PROBABILITY OF ADDICTION
LEGAL, MEDICAL AND SOCIAL IMPLICATIONS

DAVID A. PETERS

Austin & Winfield, Publishers
San Francisco - London - Bethesda
1997

Library of Congress Cataloging-in-Publication Data

Peters, David A., 1949-
    The probability of addiction : legal, medical, and social
    implications \ David A. Peters.
      p. cm.
    Includes bibliographical references and index.
    ISBN 1-57292-053-X (cloth : alk. paper). -- ISBN 1-57292-052-1
(pbk. : alk. paper)
      1. Narcotic habit—United States—Forecasting. 2. Drug abuse-
-United States—Forecasting. I. Title.
    HV5825.P39   1996
    362.29'12'097301—dc20   96-46207
                                            CIP

Editorial Inquiries:
Austin & Winfield, Publishers
7831 Woodmont Avenue #345
Bethesda, MD 20814
(301) 654-7335

To Order: (800) 99-AUSTIN

The Publisher is not responsible for any possible error in the rendering of chemical formulae or concepts.

This book is dedicated to
Phillip F. Peters
(both of them)

Foreword

David has asked me to comment on this manuscript, as a representative of the legal system and as someone who knows him and his work. I frequently see people whose families, careers, and very lives have been ruined because of their use of addicting substances, and because society seems devoid of interest in providing any real assistance to the victims of drug addiction.

My area of interest, and the majority of my remarks, focus on Chapter 3: Legal, Medical, and Social implications, but let me briefly comment on this work as a whole. This book is carefully researched, with information from older books as well as modern articles. For those not well-schooled in science or mathematics, David has provided appendices explaining basic concepts relating to the text. Although sometimes rather technical, this book does a good job of presenting and proving its premises.

As David says, there are entire libraries written about drug addiction. Why, then, should someone want another book? For one thing, this book presents a complete theory. As I understand, David's theory lets us make reasonable predictions as to who will become addicted to drugs, and which drugs are most addicting to certain people. Among all the texts I am aware of, this is a unique idea.

In Chapter 3, David argues against the legalization of addicting substances now controlled. Before reading this section, I believed these drugs should be legalized, feeling such action would cut crime, especially highly-organized crime relating to drug trafficking. Also, as a defense attorney, I am in a unique position to see what our legal system has done to drug addicts. As is often said, the war on drugs is usually just a war on people. Most people are simply too poor to obtain treatment in the best centers, or at the right time. Hence, jail or prison is the likely consequence.

The point made here is that legalization will increase the number of drug addicts, and they are David's main concern in writing this work. David and I may still have some disagreement on the issue of drug legalization, but David has made his point well. I am considering asking for the drug legalization part of this book to be published in the legal literature.

David mentions my same point in several places, with examples such as a 17-year old sentenced to ten years in prison for mailing two tablets of LSD from college to a friend at home. In a typical political frenzy, Congress has passed absurdly rigid sentencing guidelines that wreak havoc on people who are already victims of a cartel whose purpose is to make the leaders rich at any cost in huwan misery. I have seen this all too often.

What can we do? A good part of the answer may well lie in the book you are holding. If we can identify who is at risk for drug addiction, we can act to stop it before it reaches tragic proportions. The value of preemptive activity cannot be overstated. Prisons are already full, and at best are useless in rehabilitating an offender. Everyone wants harsher sentences until it is their son or daughter who is convicted. Once convicted, we are at the mercy of the government and its peculiar methods of rehabilitation. These methods are often nothing more than warehousing and retribution.

This book virtually proves that we must make changes to inner cities and society in general if we are to avert more tragedy. We must provide proper diagnosis and treatment, not additional incarceration. As David states, there are no hopeless addicts. If addiction is a dormant volcano, then hope is a dormant spring. If this theory is accepted, there is always a probability that an addict will recover. David is proof of this in a number of ways.

Fred Bruno, Esq.

Fred is a past chair of the Criminal Section of the Minnesota Bar Association. He is considered one of the top trial lawyers in the area, working out of his Minneapolis law firm Frederic Bruno & Associates. Fred teaches, writes and edits legal publications, and speaks to political groups as his time permits. And, most to his credit, he spends a lot of time in jail – assisting people like the author.

DAP

Table of Contents

Figures

Tables

Axioms

Boxes & Calculations

Trademarks

The names in the left-hand column are registered trademarks mentioned in this book. The company holding the trademark is shown in the right-hand column.

Band-Aid™	Johnson & Johnson
Black Flag™	Boyle Midway Corporation
Boone's Farm™	Ernest & Julio Gallo Winery
Darvon™	Eli Lilly and Company
Demerol™	Winthrop Pharmaceuticals
Dilaudid™	Knoll Pharmaceuticals
Empirin™	Burroughs Wellcome
Librium™	Hoffmann-La Roche
Midol™	Sterling Winthrop, Inc.
Dolophine™	Eli Lilly and Company
Ping-Pong	Parker Brothers
Preludin™	Boehringer Ingelheim
Ripple™	Ernest & Julio Gallo Winery
Starship Enterprize™	Paramount Pictures
Talwin™	Winthrop Pharmaceuticals
Twinkie(s)™	Continental Bakeries Corporation
Valium™	Hoffmann-La Roche
Xylocaine™	Astra Pharmaceutical Products

Preface

As scientific discoveries cascaded in the late Nineteenth and early Twentieth centuries, many believed we could eventually predict everything. If we knew the position and motion of every atom in the universe, the logic went, we could exactly predict the future, including huwan[1] action. Scientists have largely abandoned total prediction following the Heisenberg Uncertainty Principle and the mathematics of chaos. Even if we fully understood every particle, we could not predict who would win the next presidential race.

To some extent, however, determinism continues in the popular perception of the Huwan Genome Project. When we finish mapping all 23 huwan chromosomes, many believe, we will know everything possible about every person. This ignores the fact that DNA does not actually contain all huwan genetic information. Part of the information necessary to "construct" a huwan exists in the cellular enzymes that turn various genes on and off. (Genes ultimately determine these, too, unless cellular enzymes are passed directly to the child inside the reproductive cells of the parents.)

Imagine attaching sensitive detectors to all the printed-circuit

---

[1] Please see Appendix E for all-inclusive writing conventions.

connections coming out of a computer chip and, using a sufficiently fast device, recording every voltage change. How long would it take to figure out whether the computer was running a word processor or playing a game? Probably no known technology could integrate the torrent of information in any meaningful fashion. The deterministic prediction of huwan action ignores the complexity of a single huwan mind. There are also the interactions with the millions of minds, some no longer alive, that we call society.

Given the difficulties of predicting any complicated event such as huwan behavior, the most radical concept in this book is the claim that drug addiction can be predicted with reasonable precision. This is not the simple deterministic model described above – mechanical prediction based on knowing all positions and velocities – but the application of statistical technique to reach an acceptable confidence level.

Assuming the book makes an adequate case for my definition of addiction and its prediction, certain conclusions can be drawn. Some approaches to treating drug addiction make the problem worse, some are simply useless, and a few, almost by accident, do reduce the probability of addiction. And what does the probability theory say about the legalization of "controlled substances"? What effect would such legalization have on our society? Are individual addicts responsible for their actions? Is society responsible for perpetuating the conditions that lead to drug addiction? Chapter 3 discusses these issues.

Writing Conventions

Although I intend this book as scientific work, I have tried to make it more readable than insurance contracts and military standards. I have abandoned certain formal conventions such as "the author," "the reader," and have tried not to use too many technical writing formalities as "the following" and "utilize." Sometimes these formalities make an important distinction; then, of course, they are required.

Rhetorical researchers have prepared two passages containing *exactly* the same information. One passage was written in a simple, straightforward style, and the other was written with the convoluted jargon of the professional. Doctors, engineers, and other professionals tested report that the convoluted passage contained more information! For the benefit of the non-professional reader of this book, I hope the professionals will be tolerant.

The subject of addiction requires the use of certain technical terms. The appendices explain technical terms and concepts. Those not familiar with the basics of probability, genetics, chemistry, or the terminology of psychology, might want to read Appendix A, B, C, or D before starting Chapter 1.

There are problems with common terms and street slang for drugs. The addict may consistently use "girl" for cocaine (and then again, se[2] may not), but what se purchases may be a mixture of methamphet-

---

2 Please see Appendix E for these pronouns.

amine and caffeine (and talcum powder or rat poison, for that matter). Also, literature has propagated silly drug terminology never used by addicts: in 25 years of speaking with addicts, I have never heard the term "nose candy" used for cocaine.

This book uses the simplest chemical term for the drug, except where it is too specific. Addicts using the term "speed," for example, mean to include methamphetamine, amphetamine, and phenmetrazine. The term "speed freak" is thus more scientifically accurate than the scientific sounding "methamphetamine addict." No speed freak will ever turn down any of the three powerful stimulants mentioned.

I use quotes around "street" dosages: a speed freak (stimulant addict) reports shooting (injecting intravenously) a gram or more of "meth." A gram of pure methamphetamine would keep half the Senate awake and alert for a week (a powerful drug indeed). Addicts always misrepresent dosages, claiming excessive usage to their friends and minimal usage to their parents or the police. Careful questioning can get the addict to give an accurate measure of what se injected, but we are still left with the question of how much of what they injected is what they intended to inject.

Some material in this book requires references. The bibliography at the end of the book lists various books and articles that relate to the chapters. References are indexed by the first four letters of the author's last name followed (with no space) by the year of publication. This book, for example, would be designated PETE96. The bibliography includes not only works directly referenced in this book but also works which may contradict part of the theory presented here. Works cited in the bibliography were not used to construct the theory presented here. The ideas I am presenting came from interviews and close association with several hundred drug addicts.

Alcoholism is more popular to research and document than other drug addictions. It is probably not because addiction to ethyl alcohol is older, since ancient cultures used opium, coca leaves (cocaine), and hallucinogens. Part of the reason is probably the accessibility of ethyl alcohol: it is legal. Researchers probably have more trouble purchasing methamphetamine than most inner-city kids! Rather than "alcoholic," this book uses the broader and perhaps more-correct term "addict." Unless noted in specific cases or studies, the word "addict" always includes alcoholics in this book.[3]

Most people will find this final convention radical: use of the Gaynor Conventions (Appendix E) to replace the male-specific terms our language uses for all people. I do not want to make any heavy political point; I simply tire of writing *he or she* and *her or him*.[4] Addiction is not limited to one gender, race, or social group (although the reasons for addiction may differ for each group).

---

[3] To some hard-core Twelve-Steppers, putting alcoholics in with addicts is heresy. They are going to have to live with it: the similarities far outweigh the differences.

[4] For an individual of known sex, the pronoun representing har sex is used: the author is "he," not "se."

Introduction

Drug addiction has killed individuals, left others in a "persistent vegetative state," created violent street gangs, destroyed families, and endangered whole cultures (not just that of the United States). Why do some people continue to put a chemical substance into their bodies when they know it is killing them? (We reject Freud's death wish: if someone wants to die, there are easier methods.) It is obvious to many health-care workers, family, and friends (if any remain) that the addict is totally out of control. Not only are addicts unable to help themselves, they often fight viciously when others try to come to their aid.

In the 1980's, discovery of A1 and D2 genes linked to alcoholism promised the ultimate predictor of addiction, at least to alcohol. Or did it? Immediately, controversy started: 40 percent of alcoholics do not have the A1 gene and one third do not have D2. So, the researchers might counter, are they really alcoholics? Perhaps the study's critics used the wrong sample: D2 researchers went around the controversy by defining a new type of alcoholism (BLIM90)! What about non-addicts who carry the gene? If they take a drink, are they destined to a slow death from cirrhosis? This book seeks to answer these issues by defining active addiction and predicting who will "get" it.[5]

---

[5] GOLD71, MUEL88, SCIE88, and BOWE91 discuss the A1 and D2 genes and the inheritance of alcoholism (not necessarily valid for all drug addiction). Appendix C explains basic genetics, including how the term "gene" may be misleading in these cases.

The A1/D2 controversy is a variation on the old nature versus nurture question. Are the horrors of addiction a result of a gene or other factors in the individual? Is addiction the result of family environment and peer pressure? Is addiction "simply" an indication of deep psychological problems? As news coverage of "crack" and "ice" suggests, are some drugs so powerful that a single exposure ensures addiction? Seldom the case in school but frequently the case in real life, the answer is (e) All of the above.

Addiction is the compulsive use of a chemical substance long after the point where its consequences are apparent. Twelve-step programs and the popular conception "once an addict, always an addict" maintain that even if an addict stops using a substance, se remains an addict for life. Although this has good basis (Axiom 3), an addict, for our purposes, is a person currently abusing a chemical substance, including, of course, alcohol. Some ideas in this book may apply to addictions such as gambling, sex (PDNE87), and food, but the data came from alcoholics/drug addicts. This book deals with chemical addiction.

Factor P_a is the probability that an individual will become addicted to a chemical substance.

$$P_a := P_s + P_i \text{ (maximum of 1.00)}$$

with symbols defined as

P_a Probability of active addiction

P_s Potential of chemical substance for abuse

P_i Likelihood individual will become an addict

1. Assigning a Value to Factor P_a

Appendix A presents a formal mathematical discussion of probability and shows how I derived this formula and the others in this book. I am borrowing the symbol ":=" from the Pascal computer programming language: it means the variable on the left is assigned the value computed as on the right. Those not interested in the mathematics can read the symbol as "equals" without losing any of the meaning. Please remember, though, that adding probabilities has a specific meaning in mathematics, and I am not implying a simple sum of probabilities in these formulas.

A score of .95 means the person is "very likely" to become an addict, while a final score of .15 means there is little chance of an addiction. If factors P_i and P_s are formed properly from their constituent values, P_a should predict the incidence of addiction within the generally–accepted 5 percent confidence level. Subsequent sections reduce factors P_i and P_s

to similar, lower-level factors. Because of multiple factors, a mistake in one should not radically skew the resulting P_a value.

Chapter 2 formally defines addiction, but the brief definition just given of an alcoholic/drug addict will serve for now. As with most prejudice, the popular image of an addict as a smelly, disheveled, man inhabiting a cardboard box in an alley has some basis. What starts as fun and games with a group of friends progresses to compulsive chemical use, often in isolation. The end of addiction is "jails, institutions, and death" (NAWS87).

Using this book, it should be possible to assign working values for all the factors in the probability of addiction. Further study may require adjustment of the individual values and perhaps even the addition of a factor, but the basic idea should not change. This book presents the idea that there is a probability an individual will become addicted to a chemical substance. That probability can be found by combining factors about the individual and factors about the chemical substance to which the individual is exposed. By assigning values to factors P_i and P_s using tables in Chapters 1 and 2, we can predict the "odds" that the chemical user will become a drug addict.

Addiction Versus Use

Chapter 2 gives a formal definition of drug addiction, but I need to make certain points at this time. In the last stage of addiction, it is difficult to deny there is a problem: even the addict is aware of it. Those who most vehemently deny a problem with drugs, including ethyl alcohol, probably have some problem. This is, however, not always the case. Naturally, a person would be upset being confined in an inpatient treatment program for no good reason.

I once faced a dilemma involving a young lady whose mother had "put her in treatment." I knew her and her family well. She was attractive, socially adept, intelligent, and, to the continued dismay of her mother, flagrantly sexually active as a young teen. She had tried marijuana and drank alcohol occasionally. Calling from the treatment center, she asked if I thought she was a drug addict.

To answer "no" was to perhaps undermine the treatment staff, who work furiously to convince people they need to "surrender," "do their First Step," and so forth. To satisfy the staff, she had to admit she was an addict. She felt, however, that her mother had confined her simply because she repeatedly failed to live up to her mother's ideal for her behavior, or sometimes even minimum standards of responsibility. I had to say I did not feel she was a drug addict.

Are there political prisoners in drug treatment centers? I believe so. The medical establishment considers alcoholism a disease and many states have codified alcoholism and other addictions into statutes.

Since an employee can usually not be fired for having a disease, this reduces some personal responsibility. By alleging a drug (alcohol) problem or accepting the diagnosis of the treatment center, the person may retain har[6] job. (Drug treatment centers have a difficult job, hobbled by insurance limits, forced to change a 10-year lifestyle in a month, required to meet numerous court, state, and federal regulations.)

Only in the last stage of addiction is the addict completely out of touch with reality and perhaps unable to control har behavior. In earlier stages, the addict may be claiming insanity to obtain a lighter sentence. Treatment programs and Twelve-Step groups such as Alcoholics Anonymous appropriately say, "We are not responsible for our disease, but we are responsible for our recovery."

(Drug *possession* is a difficult call. Having a drug, by itself, does not harm anyone but the addict. Does a mandatory sentence of 10 years in prison do less harm? Does it help society in any way to create a being adept only at surviving in a criminal environment? Nevertheless, we cannot continue to allow people to absorb chemicals which seriously impair reflexes and judgment and then operate automobiles. Chapter 3 deals with these issues.)

Everyone who uses a drug is not an addict, at least not yet. This is a the difficult part of the work for drug treatment counselors. A client smoked marijuana while operating a locomotive and was "placed in treatment" as a condition of further employment with the railroad. A counselor tells the engineer, "Perhaps you're not in danger yet, but

---

6   See Appendix E for the conventions on non-sexist language.

suppose you are on a train for Chicago. If you do not get off the train at some point, you will arrive in Chicago." Such constant (and rather brilliant!) battering by the staff is designed to break down the defenses of the addict. What effect it might have on a non-addict should probably be examined.

Some older members of Alcoholics Anonymous took a different tack. When a young member stated at a meeting that se was unsure if se was an alcoholic, the experienced members smiled and replied, "Well, kid, why don't you go out and get into some more trouble. Come back when you are sure." Some of these more-experienced members had lost their homes, family, teeth, liver, and every gram of self respect to ethyl alcohol. They did not feel like listening to excuses.

So how do we decide whether someone is destined to become a drug addict or is simply engaged in adolescent experimentation? The probability concept of addiction is intended to provide as good an answer as possible (probable?). If our experimenter is exposed to a sufficiently powerful chemical substance (Chapter 1) and has certain personal and social characteristics (Chapter 2), addiction is probable.

I hope the concepts presented here provide a basis for developing appropriate tests and interviews to find who is at risk. Drug addiction is like other medical conditions: the best way to treat it is to prevent its onset. Where addiction has occurred, we need to correctly diagnose it and provide appropriate treatment. Finally, I hope this probability concept fosters an accurate, scientific, and humane way for society to view drug addiction.

Chapter 1
Addicting Chemicals

The ability of a chemical to addict someone is a combination of factors. A chemical substance must meet the requirements of Axiom 1. In addition, the effect of the drug must be pleasurable or desirable in

$$P_s := P_c + P_r + P_p$$

with symbols defined as

P_c Addiction potential of chemical

P_r Route of administration

P_p Perception of drug effect

2. Assigning a Value to Factor P_s

some way. This depends partially on how it is administered and how the potential addict perceives the effects.

Chapter 2 covers the characteristics of the person taking the drug; the present chapter concerns the addicting chemical substance. The P_s

box shows the formula for the probability of a substance being addicting.

This chapter covers each factor as if they were entirely distinct, which, of course, is not true. (See "Independent Events" in Appendix A.) The nature of the substance affects the perception of it and limits the route of administration. It is difficult, for example, to inject nitrous oxide or marijuana and hard to smoke ethyl alcohol. Factors not even in this equation such as the environment (Chapter 2) affect the perception. Ignoring contributions from other factors, perception probably overrides everything and should perhaps be weighted (the p subscript might also stand for "placebo effect").

The distinction between physical and psychological dependence, if it exists at all, is of no value in predicting the likelihood of addiction. Before 1980, everyone (except the addicts) maintained that heroin was "truly" addicting while cocaine was merely psychologically addicting. In the 1980's, the lay press, opposing current scientific thought, labeled "crack" the most addicting substance known. What really are the differences between heroin addiction and cocaine addiction? Addicts lied, cheated, prostituted themselves for either drug. Abrupt withdrawal of either drug following months of continuous use caused pain sufficient to keep the addict acting in ways undesirable even to the addict. Chapter 2 covers psychological addiction: at this point, assume all addiction is "real."

Definition of Addicting Chemical

This subsection gives the characteristics a chemical substance must have to be addicting. This condition is necessary but not sufficient. As later subsections show, the substance must not only be able to produce an addiction (by Axiom 1), it must also have some effect the addict wants. Later subsections examine this effect; Chapter 2 shows the characteristics of the individuals that are especially subject to these effects.

Axiom 1
Any addicting substance replaces a chemical substance produced naturally by the huwan body.

Corollary
Any substance that can replace a chemical naturally produced by the huwan body has the potential to be addicting.

The foreign substance may have a direct chemical analog in the huwan body (although finding it is the stuff of which Nobel prizes are made). Research in the 1970's showed such a direct relationship by linking opiates such as heroin, morphine, and codeine with the brain receptors for endorphins, the brain's natural painkillers. The relationship may be more circuitous, consistent with complicated feedback machinery in the huwan body. Such a mechanism is seen in cocaine addiction: cocaine binds to the re-uptake mechanism for l-dopamine. Cocaine does not strictly replace dopamine, but in the presence of cocaine, the body does not deplete the intercellular (systemic) supply of dopamine and therefore does not produce more. (PERT73, SIMO73)

Starting with Axiom 1, the mechanism of physical addiction is simple (Figure 1). The addict regularly injects heroin. The heroin binds to sites normally used by α-enkephalins (a form of endorphin). The body's exquisitely balanced feedback mechanism senses there is plenty of α-enkephalin and quits producing it. If the addict uses high-quality heroin for even a month, the body's ability to produce enkephalins diminishes: the production mechanism atrophies. If the addict stops using suddenly, se experiences a pain outside the realm of ordinary experience.

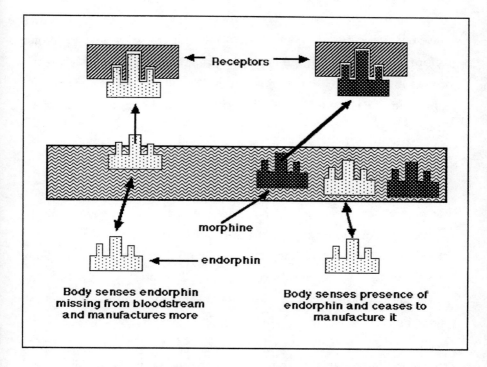

Figure 1. Direct (Simplest) Mechanism of Addiction

Axiom 1 implies that many substances are addicting. Have you ever used a Chap-Stick™ for an extended time and stopped abruptly? The effects of dry, cracked lips, for which the substance was originally used, were then multiplied tenfold. This is the same withdrawal effect seen with heroin, cocaine, and amphetamines. The body requires time after the substance is no longer available to begin producing the natural product. Much of the addicts' pain and seeming impatience with the world, including anhedonia, is due to this.

Lysergic acid diethylamide-25 (LSD) radically alters the balance of neurotransmitter 5-hydroxytryptamine (serotonin). The LSD leaves the body very quickly compared to most drugs: it is virtually gone before the main part of the hallucinogenic trip. (Dealing with quantities as minute as 100 micrograms, it is difficult to say the LSD is "all" gone, but it has been detected in urine several hours after ingestion. The peak of the trip is six to eight hours after ingestion.) What, then, does LSD replace?

By this theory of addiction, LSD replaces whatever factor(s) account for normal serotonin production. This may be a mixture of chemicals in the brain or the result of outside stimuli that cause neurons to fire, stimulate an associative tract, and eventually produce serotonin (both are fundamentally chemical events). LSD does not replace serotonin, but it does replace whatever feedback mechanism controls the serotonin balance within the brain. The LSD user experiences greatly accelerated mental (dis)functioning, believes harself extremely creative, and sometimes "senses" things that are not even there (hallucinations). When a chronic LSD user is not "high," se feels mentally deficient, lethargic, indifferent and appears tired, stupid, and unmotivated to an observer. The tripper is now addicted and requires the substance.

Alcohol has widespread effects on brain chemicals; the exact substance(s) replaced may have to wait for improved technology in the area of brain function. Axiom 1 predicts such chemicals will be found. The relationship is not as obvious as that of opiates replacing endorphins, but it is there. Alcohol is addicting: stopping access to the substance in a longtime user produces a severe, sometimes even fatal, withdrawal syndrome that includes delirium tremens.

When I began this book in 1991, no one had released information about any definite brain chemical replaced by tetrahydrocannabinol (THC), the active ingredient in marijuana. Such a chemical has now been found; it has been nicknamed anandamine, from the Sanskrit word *ananda*, meaning "bliss." Such a receptor was "predicted" when researchers found a protein receptor that binds to THC in 1988. The receptor, of course, evolved for a reason: though the chemical had not been isolated, this receptor implied the huwan brain produced a marijuana-like chemical (FACK93).

Marijuana addicts lose short term memory and motivation, making the drug an effective anesthetic for a bad life situation (also see Chapter 2). Although the media does not associate "cravings" with marijuana as with cocaine and amphetamines, users do report such feelings. It is readily apparent from any population of addicts that relapse rates for marijuana users are just as high as those for cocaine.

Marijuana is dangerous, for individuals and society. This addicting drug destroys motivation: all desire to and attempts at improving one's life. The fact that it does not share all the overt consequences of drug abuse – an abscess, collapsed veins, overdose, AIDS – makes it even more dangerous: the addict can falsely regard har marijuana use as "safe." More often than regarding drug use as safe, however, addicts simply do not care about consequences, if they have even bothered to think things through to that point. This apathy is certainly attenuated by use of the drug marijuana.

Addiction Potential (P$_c$)

Chemicals commonly abused by huwan beings – natural and synthetic narcotics, amphetamines and substitutes, cocaine, many hallucinogens, and phencyclidine (PCP)–are used by every animal so far tested. Given the opportunity, the animals continue to take the drug once it has started (JOHA76). Most huwan cultures use some form of an addicting chemical: peyote, coca leaves, fermented brews (ethyl alcohol), opium, tobacco, and caffeine products. Perhaps this is the origin of the theory expounded by some famous drug proponents such as Dr. Timothy Leary that people have some inherent need to alter consciousness. Evidence indicates that some substances have a high potential for creating drug addiction and some individuals in all populations are vulnerable to such addiction.

Table 1 shows the commonly accepted classification of addiction potential for some abused substances. This is only of historical interest: as stated above, the distinctions are virtually meaningless as far as probability of addiction. If the addict continues to use the subst ance–whatever the reason – the substance is addicting. A hierarchical list is possible (or else P$_s$ would be meaningless), but we must be very careful about the criteria used order the list. LSD, for example, does not produce tolerance as seen with heroin; after a half dozen 800 mcg. LSD trips in a row, no amount of LSD will produce the desired effect again. If, however, we use mental derangement as a criterion, an addict on 800 mcg. of LSD is much more incapacitated than an addict on 80 mg. of heroin.

Table 1. Common Addiction Potentials (most incorrect)

I. Physically Addicting	
heroin	morphine
hydromorphone (Dilaudid)	meperidine (Demerol)
II. Psychologically Addicting	
phenmetrazine (Preludin)	methamphetamine
cocaine	marijuana
lysergic acid diethylamide (LSD)	mescaline
III. Habituating (not addictive)	
alcohol	codeine
propoxyphene (Darvon)	pentazocine (Talwin)
diazepam (Valium)	
IV. Mildly Habit Forming	
caffeine	
	nicotine (cigarettes)

If the Table 1 hierarchy were correct, we could directly assign probabilities of addiction to each category: $P_I = .5$, $P_{II} = .4$, $P_{III} = .3$, and so forth. Though the difference between psychological and physical addiction is virtually meaningless, there is nonetheless a difference between drugs. One difference is in etiology: some drugs take longer to destroy the addict than others do. Given unlimited access to marijuana, the addict might live for decades and might even do something productive during the first six months. Given unlimited access to methamphetamine, the addict could die within a year, with all productivity ending after the first week.

A more accurate hierarchy of addiction potential is given in Table 2. Table 2 is more "accurate" because it better reflects the ability of the substance to cause a person to continue compulsive use. Further research may indicate two factors are required to define the addiction potential: initial satisfaction and persistence of effect, for example. (Appendix B briefly explains concepts like *potency* and *efficacy* that relate to a drug's ability to addict.)

Table 2 does not list all substances: neither does the Federal Registry nor the Government's Controlled Substance categories, nor probably even the Physician's Desk Reference (PDRE91). New psychoactive drugs are discovered, and addicts find or invent new addicting chemicals. Substances not listed can be classified by comparison with a related substance in the table. Mescaline, for example, belongs with LSD and fentanyl belongs with hydromorphone.

Caffeine and nicotine, listed as "not always addicting," have more addicts than all other substances combined. In a typical neurotic circle, this effect becomes an additional cause. The fact that caffeine and nicotine are widespread and socially acceptable increases the probability that someone will become addicted to them. Both substances are extensively advertised, even though nicotine is poisonous in any quantity to anyone not already addicted. The hypocrisy of legal cigarettes, lying tobacco companies, and glamorous alcohol ads is not lost on teenagers. They are also unlikely to listen to an anti-drug tirade by drunk parents with cigarettes hanging out of their mouths.

However widespread the addiction, first use of nicotine is virtually always a bad experience and many people instinctively find the taste of coffee offensive. Teenagers see parents and friends "enjoying" these substances (requiring them is probably accurate). They see the myriad advertisements, including use by actors and actresses, and then receive support from their friends for trying them. Once advertisers and society's addicts get an addiction-prone person to try an addicting substance – even an offensive substance such as nicotine – an active addiction is likely to occur. (Also see "Perception of Drug Effect.")

Table 2. Realistic Addiction Potentials

Any Exposure Dangerous (Pc = .30)	
cocaine	phenmetrazine (Preludin®)
methamphetamine	heroin
morphine	
High Addiction Potential: Pc = .25	
hydromorphone (Dilaudid®)	meperidine (Demerol®)
benzedrine/dexadrine	
Moderate Addiction Potential: Pc = .20	
ethyl alcohol	propoxyphene (Darvon®)
pentazocine (Talwin®)	diazepam (Valium®)
all barbiturates	lysergic acid diethylamide (LSD)
Addiction Requires Repeated Exposure: P_c = .15	
Nicotine (cigarettes)	Caffeine (coffee, tea, colas)

Route of Administration (P_a)

How the substance is administered can radically alter the hierarchy of Table 2: injected pentazocine probably has a higher addiction potential than heroin administered orally. Some individuals maintain they would never take an illegal drug; some who smoke marijuana swear they would never use "hard drugs," by which they usually mean something that is ordinarily injected. Obvious physical differences play some part in deciding how a drug is used; as mentioned, it is hard to inject marijuana or smoke alcohol, but the ingenuity of addicts for getting drugs into their systems is legendary.

When selecting the method to get drugs into the body, an important factor is what "everyone else" is doing. One addict, originally "scared to death of needles," became adept at injecting himself with meperidine. He would keep the needle in his arm until his eyes rolled back in his head and he lost consciousness. The fear of injections was insufficient to even slow the progress of the addiction.

Addicts sometimes claim they often smoke dope (marijuana), but would never use "hard drugs." When pressed for a definition of hard drugs, they usually mention "needles" (syringes). This is probably a peer influence, not a matter of conscience or upbringing. If literally everyone around the potential addict (someone with high P_i) were injecting heroin, that person would also inject heroin.

Pharmacology distinguishes between the potency of a substance (the physical quantity required to achieve an effect) and the efficacy (the level of desired effect achievable with that substance). Both efficacy and potency are relevant to addiction potential. The efficacy, effectiveness for altering the addict's mood in some desirable fashion, and not the potency, determines the hierarchy of Table 2 (or Table 1, for that matter).

Potency is relevant because a junkie would not like to shoot two pints of liquid to get high. Speed freaks "cook down" (evaporate the liquid in) their hit to increase the "rush" (the initial shock to the nervous system). Although efficacy cannot be changed without changing the chemical substance, potency can be effectively altered by route of administration.

Variations in potency present an ever-present danger to many addicts because of the unpredictability of street drugs. Used to injecting several dime bags (about half a teaspoon of very low quality heroin, costing $20) at once, the addict accidentally obtains some heroin not yet cut (adulterated) dozens of times. A half teaspoon of pure heroin would kill anyone, even an addict. Similarly, the addict might obtain a drug such as α-methyl-fentanyl with potency and efficacy both greater than that of heroin. The result may be the same.

A television report identified crack as "a highly addictive form of cocaine." "Crack" is not different from cocaine; it is the most addictive form by only a slight margin, if at all. Appendix B examines the chemistry of cocaine (and several other drugs) and distinguishes between the "base" form and the crystalline powder. This so-called base form is "crack."

Cocaine reaches the brain twice as fast from inhaling "crack" vapor as from injection of cocaine hydrochloride (JONE88). This means the "rush" is more rapid when the cocaine is vaporized and inhaled. Amphetamine users are seen with sores, bruises, and abscesses all over their arms, but seldom on their legs. Injection of a stimulant in veins of the legs causes a delay in the drug's reaching the brain and dilutes the immediate effect of the drug (the rush).

I do not plan on testing it, but I believe the plague of smoked cocaine in the form of crack is due to the minimum skill and equipment required. If injection were made equally easy, such as by placing a catheter in an arm vein, many addicts would choose IV injection over inhalation. Without such empirical evidence, however, I rate inhalation as high as intravenous administration in Box 3.

Factor P_r is assigned values depending on how quickly the chemical reaches an effective concentration. This factor partially accounted for another important factor: how much of the drug reaches its intended target (some brain receptor). An addict who has collapsed or abscessed veins in both arm veins might inject the stimulant into a vein in the leg or foot.[7] Usually, the alternate route is found satisfactory and the addiction continues.

---

7 Narcotics do not give the as sharp a "rush" as stimulants such as methamphetamine and cocaine. Injecting them into an arm vein is not as important. The delay, however, is dangerous. Because of the immense impact of an injection of methamphetamine, it is difficult to overdose: the user cannot even see well enough to manage the injection. It is quite possible, however, to inject enough heroin into a leg vein to cause death.

Intravenous injection	.10
Vaporization by heat and inhalation	.10
Inhalation of vapor	.09
Intramuscular injection	.06
Inhalation of powder	.05
Oral ingestion	.03

3. Assigning a Value to Factor P_r

Inhalation of vapor refers to abuse of substances such as toluene (present in glue for plastics), benzene, chloroform, diethyl ether, gasoline, various thinners and aerosol propellants. This is perhaps the most damaging of all drug abuse. Vaporization by heat and inhalation includes all substances smoked: marijuana, crack cocaine, and nicotine are common examples. Note that there is a danger in altering the chemical by this process. During a "thin period" when he could not obtain sufficient marijuana, one addict smoked freshly-ground coffee. He said he expectorated a yellowish phlegm for months afterward.

A special warning should be made about inhaling solvents. Current law recognizes some controlled substances as having medical uses and some as having no medical use. This – and not the addiction potential – is the basis of the Schedule I and II controlled substance classifications according to law. Inhaled chemicals such as gasoline and toluene are not only of no medical use, they are classified as poisons. These substances do terrible damage to those who abuse them and do it very quickly. Although they are not controlled substances, solvents and fuels such as butane and gasoline should perhaps be considered "Schedule 0" drugs.

An important drug effect is the type of reinforcement drugs provide. (Readers not familiar with reinforcement schedules should see Appendix D before continuing. This concept is important in understanding how the drugs reward users so effectively.) Since the reinforcement from a drug can occur very quickly, it reinforces the user in at a basic, animal level. A lasting high and other secondary rewards like camaraderie also reinforce the drug user.

The great behaviorist B. F. Skinner could not have designed a better system than drug abuse for causing a behavior to persist. In early stages of addiction, the user is rewarded – immediately and highly effectively – for taking the substance. As se gains tolerance for the drug, the rush occurs on an erratic schedule, depending not only on the physical condition of the addict but also the quality of the drug. Injecting drugs is a fine example of Dr. Skinner's variable interval reinforcement schedule.

The reward of the "rush" occurs almost every time at first, due to the lesser tolerance of the addict for the drug. When use of the drug gets to be a lifestyle, reinforcement is intermittent. Purity varies. Suppliers of the drug are jailed. The health of the user is deteriorating. Reinforcement is given, but not every time.

In Stage 3 of addiction, the drug may even make the addict sick (not the transient nausea of some narcotics, but hours of regurgitating green bile). Expecting ever-increasing tolerance, the addict continues increasing the dose, but har system may no longer be able to handle even a small quantity of the drug. The liver, for example, may not be able to handle the breakdown of the drug due to extensive damage and possibly hepatitis. A small additional amount of the substance effectively poisons the addict.

Since the desired effect is still occasionally achieved, the negative reinforcement of the sickness may be a more effective reinforcement schedule than the variable interval schedule (Appendix D). Sickness that accompanies the drug may actually make the behavior of drug use harder to extinguish! The addict in effect learns to take much pain in the pursuit of the drug high.

A behavior reinforced with the awesome power of a rush from injecting drugs and on a variable-interval reinforcement schedule can probably never be counteracted: strong electric shock will not stop drug use. We see this phenomenon as the "needle freaks": addicts who inject magnesium sulfate (Epsom salts), Ripple[8], oil from peanut butter, Black Flag insecticide, and even cold tap water in an attempt to experience a rush. It is sometimes their last.

---

8 "Ripple" and "Boone's Farm" are inexpensive wines manufactured by Ernest & Julio Gallo. Although either name may be used by addicts as a generic term for cheap wine, E & J Gallo deserve the credit for introducing the words.

Perception of Drug Effect (P_p)

An injection of 100 mg. of methamphetamine or 200 mg. of phenmetrazine (both as hydrochloride) causes an immediate cold sensation in the chest, as with a breath of freezing air. Simultaneously, there is a sensation of expanding, coupled with sensory alterations: tunnel vision, hearing sounds as if the user were in a well, proprioceptive changes that seem to loosen all muscles and expand cells. Physiologically, heart rate triples, pupils become almost totally dilated, breathing can stop for several minutes. This is a totally inadequate description of the sought-after rush.

The immediate effects of an injection of "speed" are extremely powerful. The closest a "layperson" might get to understanding it is to imagine drinking 75 cups of very strong coffee in less than a second and then jumping out of an airplane. Although one addict reported sensations of smelling burning flesh and "knowing" parts of his brain had been destroyed, the effects are generally perceived as pleasurable. Some of this perception occurs because the speed alters parts of the limbic system, causing the euphoria typically associated with narcotics. Much of it, however, is due to fellow speed freaks, without whose support, the effects might be seen as terrifying (BECK67 and Chapter 2 of this text).

After the rush, the speed user is extremely excited, talking agitatedly and perhaps constantly. When it is physically possible, se gets up from the floor or chair and runs around getting drinks, moist towels, or cigarettes for the next person who has injected and is still unable to walk. The person appears in control, extremely happy, and very friendly, with no ulterior motive. (When the jubilant user becomes an addict, all this changes.)

Perhaps as much as half the effect of methamphetamine or phenmetrazine is learned, with the remaining part being physiological action of the drugs directly on various receptors and indirectly by initiating release of neurotransmitters. The neophyte "speed" injector learns that the experience is extremely pleasurable by watching other users. This is aided by their constant, compulsive attention: "Wow, look at har! Is se ever high, or what?" The user may have never enjoyed such fanatical attention.

Imagine that an impressionable teenager is kidnaped from a Baghdad hotel and taken to a private cell of Sadaam Hussein. After several days of hearing others screaming in agony, the teenager is interrogated. Har clothes are torn off and se is strapped in a chair with zinc tacked over the arms and seat so the blood can be cleaned off easily. Dr. Mengele comes in with a syringe and injects 100 mg. of methamphetamine into median basilic vein of har left arm. Might har perception of the experience be different from that of the high school senior who watches har friends enjoy shooting speed?[9]

To produce "drug-seeking behavior" to the point it destroys an addict's life, a substance must do more than replace a natural substance in the body. The substance must "do something" for the addict. We

---

9 I do not believe this is a strong effect with the highly addicting substances such as methamphetamine and heroin. These substances have euphoria as a main effect: the user must feel good. There is no choice. The effect, however, is important with hallucinogens – as in the "bad trip" of LSD fame.

see "euphoria" as a side effect of narcotic and stimulant drugs in the PDR (PHYS91). Euphoria is a desirable state, but the addict may also consider "agitation and excitement" desirable. Some addicts are aware of exactly the drug effect they desire. Others claim they take the drug "to get high" and, whatever that is, one drug may do it for them better than others.

Compare, for example, the physiological effects of caffeine to the powerful prescription drug prednisone, an anti-inflammatory steroid given for lupus, tissue rejection, and chronic hepatitis. (Caffeine's effects are relatively weak, but not inconsequential. See Appendix B.) Prednisone replaces the natural steroid cortisol produced by the adrenal glands. After years of use, the adrenal glands atrophy and are unable to produce cortisol. Abrupt cessation of prednisone can be fatal. Up to a year after proper withdrawal, patients must restart prednisone therapy in cases of severe trauma such as major surgery.

Although abrupt withdrawal from prednisone can be fatal, no one to my knowledge has ever been shot in a drugstore robbery where the thief's target was prednisone. Conversely, withdrawal from caffeine is not life threatening. Nevertheless, one third of the United States is addicted to caffeine in the form of coffee, tea, and numerous "soft" drinks. Caffeine can cause insomnia, headaches, constant stomach and bowel problems, and it is expensive.

Why is there such a difference between dependence on prednisone and addiction to caffeine? (Notice that even the terms used to describe long-term use of each are different.) Caffeine has strong mood-altering effects; usually, prednisone does not. In the words of an addict who had to take prednisone for hepatitis, "it doesn't do a damn thing."

There is a very strange process of addiction, involving a normally poisonous substance. The first use of nicotine is never pleasurable (except to the unethical tobacco industry). The first cigarette will make the young user cough uncontrollably, inducing dizziness and nausea. The secondary reward is sociological: the peer pressure to "fit in" accompanied by laughter of har associates at the discomfort of this rite of passage. With continued use, tolerance and true addiction to nicotine soon result.

The value of P_p depends on the number of people recommending the drug and the enthusiasm of their recommendation. A precise number would allow for the potential addict's perception of another's euphoria, perhaps a difficult thing to measure. Anecdotal evidence is not only allowed here, it is preferable. It is not necessary to measure something such as facial expressions of peers, since it is the potential addict's perception that is being quantified in P_p. The perception of drug effect is calculated from the number of highly enthusiastic peer recommendations the potential addict receives for the drug.

$$P_p := .05 \text{ x Number of Advocates}$$
$$\text{(maximum value of .25)}$$

4. Assigning a Value to Factor P_p

The advocate can be any respected source of information. The parents or surrogates who raise a child are seen in the eyes of a child as competent, superior beings and these adults, willingly or otherwise, frequently advocate drug use. (Parents should not always believe the rebelliousness children express: the child will learn from the adult, whether or not either one wants it!) An important peer, friend or respected rival, is an excellent advocate, for or against drug use. The supposed role models of society are probably not the strongest of such advocates.

The limit of five advocates for drug use is consistent with the average teenager's perception that "everyone is doing it." On thorough questioning, "everyone" is usually three or four influential people. Modern ad campaigns are attacking the idea that not everyone is getting high: this is an excellent approach to lowering the probability of addiction (PART90).

Factor P_p can have a negative value: the role model can be an advocate against drug use. Health care workers might use this by being extremely careful what they say when giving drugs such as morphine. The difference between "This will make you feel a lot better!" and "You may feel a little nausea from this" can lower the probability of addiction.

(I have seen medical staff give an injection of normal saline to a patient claiming, loudly, it was "time for har shot." It is a bad idea to give a placebo with a little pep talk in place of morphine: the person is still being taught to rely on an external substance to quell pain. Give the appropriate painkiller, when it is needed by the individual, not at the convenience of the staff or the recommendation of a doctor called away by the golf course. One more injection than what is typically considered medically necessary will not significantly increase the probability of addiction. Unless an extensive history indicates otherwise, patient behavior in a crisis is not indicative of addiction.)

Note that P_p is determined by the environmental factors that make the drug attractive. There are also factors in the environment that the drug user wants to avoid, making the relative insensitivity of the drugged state more attractive. Chapter 2 covers this escape factor.

Chapter 2
Addiction-Prone
Individuals

One addict told of his roommate who was preparing to leave for work on the night shift and complained of a headache. The addict gave him several tablets of a narcotic drug. The next day, the roommate cheerfully thanked the addict, saying "Wow, my headache went away right after I took those pills. I had a great time at work!" The roommate never mentioned the drugs again.

In relating the story, the addict said, "There is no way I would've stopped there–if my roommate had given me those pills, I would have asked for more and stolen them if he didn't give them to me." Since this was related by a person already addicted to drugs, we do not know if he might have responded differently before his addiction. Even before he took any mood-altering substance, the odds were probably always against him.

How does the deck of chemicals become stacked against someone? Although it says the same thing, we might ask this in a more scientific fashion before we try to answer it. What increases the probability that an individual, if exposed to an addicting substance as defined in Chapter 1, will become addicted to that substance? This chapter is intended to answer this in a predictive manner.

$$P_i := P_g + P_m + P_e$$

with symbols defined as

P_g	Genetic and physical factors
P_m	Mental/psychological problems
P_e	Environmental, sociological factors conducive to addiction

---

5. Assigning a Value to Factor P_i

We need at least three factors to predict the likelihood of an individual becoming an addict (P_i): genetic, mental, and environmental.

As with the addicting substance, these factors are highly interrelated, even though we must separate them to achieve any results. A single factor does not cause addiction, even if it is a large factor. For example, a war is a terribly stressful event, yet there were few addicts (including alcoholics) in World War II while one third of the Vietnam soldiers were addicted to something. Some of this has been blamed on the younger mean age for Vietnam soldiers, but I believe most of the effect is because the Vietnam War communicated no clear goals and was morally indefensible. (The second section following covers the environmental, including political, contributions to addiction.)

Definition of Addiction

So far, we have defined an addict as a person who compulsively uses a chemical substance to the point where harmful effects result. Many of these terms are moot: some addicts admit compulsive use, but most deny it even while they are injecting right beside an egg-sized abscess. For a Vice President of Chrysler, "harmful" could mean a reprimand at work; for a street addict, it might mean the sixth prison sentence. Addiction needs a more formal definition.

Axiom 2

Addiction is the point at which a chemical is taken not so much for the pleasurable effects, but because the user requires the substance to function normally.

The addict may still report that the effect is pleasurable, and, indeed, relief from withdrawal probably is one of the most pleasurable experiences. To an observer, however, the differences are obvious. A friend who is very talkative after a cup of espresso is a drug (caffeine) user. The executive who "is no good at all till I've had my coffee" is providing a good definition of drug *addiction*.

An addict who belonged to a Texas group of speed freaks known as "the barn" reported that after a year of massive use of methamphetamine paid for by prostitution, she could not get off her cot at all. Another person, had to inject her with a "gram" of methamphetamine just to get her up and functioning. At that time, she actually required methamphetamine to function: it was no longer taken to induce euphoria. During addiction, the body's mechanism for producing a needed substance atrophies as the normal substance is replaced by the chemical (Axiom 1).

The process of addiction occurs in several stages (see Box 6). Stage 1 begins when the addiction-prone individual is exposed to an appropriate substance. At this point, the user feels se can "take it or leave it." (This, of course, is debatable: if $P_a > .75$, the chances of "leaving" it are not good.) In middle stage, the person uses the substance regularly and begins to center har life around it. Friends and environment are chosen to be conducive with use of the drug. One alcoholic reported he went fishing not to catch fish but so he could sit out on the water and drink for hours without his wife nagging him.

A drug user in Stage 2 has the classic signs of addiction: increasing tolerance to the drug, extreme changes in mood, loss of interest in school and family, perhaps trouble with the law. The addict is beginning to require the chemical and is losing control. Addicts at this stage have many excellent excuses of why they are different: they need the chemical, they are in constant pain, no one understands them, the world is just too screwed up. Many addicts never make it past this stage: they are stopped by intervention (law, family, work), they simply cannot get enough of the drug, or they die of overdose attempting to counteract the tolerance.

Stage 1

- sees the drug as helpful and stress-relieving; using it is still fun
- has not changed friends and associates
- hides use from authorities but brags of it to selected friends

Stage 2

- begins to have problems: missed work and appointments, fights with family members
- changes friends, to those who also use the drug
- is very defensive about drug use
- shows tolerance to addicting substance
- starts taking other drugs to counteract effects of har drug of choice

Stage 3

- needs the drug; can barely function without it
- has few friends; associates all deal or use drugs
- stops making excuses for taking drugs
- may lose tolerance, becoming sick from small doses of drug of choice
- wants to quit and has probably tried several times
- sees life is falling apart: divorce, job loss, bankruptcy
- likely to have been hospitalized or jailed, perhaps several times
- has extensive medicine chest: stimulants, alcoholic drinks, sleeping potions, painkillers

6. Three Stages of Drug Addiction

In Stage 3, the addict probably resembles the popular nightmare: dirty and unkept, living from one bottle or fix to the next. Those who inject barbiturates now have large abscesses on their arms. The once gregarious speed freaks now allow no one into their house because of their paranoia. (In the 1970's, it was rumored that a well-known motorcycle gang helped rid California's Sunset Strip of speed freaks because these paranoid amphetamine addicts sometimes shot motorcyclists thinking they were police.) The marijuana or LSD user has no ability to concentrate: their conversation is disjointed and answers, slow in coming, may have nothing to do with the question.

The theory of cognitive dissonance says people cannot long profess one thing while doing another. In the last stage, the addict is unable to give up the drug and reduces the dissonance by ceasing to offer excuses for har behavior. The addiction has won. We see massive damage to and even failure of physical systems. This is the point of decreasing tolerance, perhaps because the badly-damaged liver can no longer metabolize the drug and more gets into and remains in the bloodstream. One drink or an ordinarily inadequate injection may result in overdose: vertigo, nausea, or, especially with cocaine, immediate death (JONE88, VOLK90).

Genetic and Physical Factors (P_g)

The A1 gene was discovered in the 1980's and, with much debate, was linked to alcoholism. There is also indirect evidence for a genetic component, showing alcoholics respond differently to alcohol. The A1 gene transcribes a protein that affects the ability of the brain to use dopamine: the gene affects the number of dopamine receptors and thus the brain's efficiency to use dopamine. The debate at this point centers around the finding that some chronic alcoholics do not have the gene and some non-alcoholics do have it. This is easily explained by the mechanism of this paper: if the A1 gene is present, the probability of addiction is increased, but not guaranteed; if the gene is absent, the probability of addiction is decreased, but not eliminated.

Suppose a family with the addiction gene (see Appendix C) belonged to a religion that permitted no exposure to addicting substances: $P_s = 0$ and most factors comprising P_i are likely to be low (a strong religious faith can produce a well-integrated individual or a fanatic: neither is a probable candidate for addiction). When a teenager abandons such faith and moves into the "enlightened" society where it seems everyone is using drugs (P_e is high), se has both motive and opportunity. It is easy to predict the result.

Uncle Henry dies of cirrhosis after years of boozing: does this indicate alcoholism in the family? Since Uncle Henry's addiction resulted from many factors, he may or may not have the proper allele of the A1 gene. As far back as the best anthropologist could trace, Mary has no alcoholics or drug addicts in her family, why has she been in three drug treatments for heroin use? It is possible (even probable) to have the proper gene for addiction and still never have an addict in the family. At the other extreme, addicts occur as a "mutation" in families with no history of drug addiction.

These seeming contradictions are easily explained by our probability concept. (They are equally well explained by assuming there is no genetic basis for drug addiction!) It is possible, and even quite probable, to have the proper gene for addiction and still never have an addict in the family. If other factors are high enough, it is also quite possible to have an addict in a family with no genetic predisposition to addiction.

Although science is not yet certain about the specific gene or genes involved in addiction, alcohol addiction is believed to "run in families." Anecdotal evidence and even early scientific studies suffered from the flaw of confusing learned coping behavior with genetics. Later work, such as twin studies, seems to show a link.

P_g is given a value of .20 for anyone with a clear incidence of addiction in their biological family. P_e, to be discussed shortly, also assigns a probability for an addictive family environment. (Note that P_e may also add to the probability of addiction for an abusive family environment.)

There are other physical mechanisms that may lead to addiction. A baby born to a mother addicted to heroin or cocaine suffers severe withdrawal symptoms. Is the child a potential addict?

One young man with type 1 (insulin dependent) diabetes suffered impaired circulation and possible nerve damage. Fearing possible gangrene, his physician hospitalized him. As he experienced severe and constant pain in his arms and legs, morphine was prescribed. In a humane attempt to limit the use of morphine, the physician ordered he was to receive it only when he asked (not on a regular schedule). This meant the young man had to "beg" for his shot, sometimes waiting at the mercy of the busy nursing staff. This variable interval reinforcement schedule taught him that after enough pain, he would receive an injection. This young man became addicted to painkillers: he was still using them years after the diabetes was under control.

Caution is in order here, least we mistake the result for the cause. At some point in har career, almost every drug addict on the planet believes se is somehow different, with some major, undiagnosed illness that absolutely requires the use of mood-altering medication. This is, in fact, precisely true, but the mysterious illness is drug addiction, not an "underlying pathological condition." Giving mood-altering drugs to a drug addict serves only to foster addiction. Chapter 3 gives some hints about treating medical problems in addicts.

Mental/Psychological Factors (P_m)

Entire books have been written about the mental problems of those who "take drugs." Psychiatrists have made careers of psychoanalyzing drug addicts, in spite of an indefensible relapse rate. There is a critical distinction between treating addiction and treating mental problems in the addict. Curing addiction by psychotherapy is like trying to program a broken computer: the therapist might be able to work around the hardware fault with some temporary success, but it simply is not possible to restore "normal" functioning in a drug addict.

(While psychotherapy is of little use while the addiction is going on, the treatment of underlying mental problems may be of great value once the person is completely drug free. Since this book defines an addict as one who is dependent on a chemical substance, "getting off" the chemical removes the addiction. Psychotherapy can be of benefit to the former addict. In spite of methadone programs requirement that clients attend "group," talk therapy for an (active) addict is like putting a Band-Aid on the San Andreas Fault.)

By the final stage, addiction has become such a problem that all other problems on earth are irrelevant. Aversion therapy involving painful electric shock is ineffective against drug-seeking behavior. While results are still inconclusive with cigarettes (RAWM90), it does not work against alcohol use (RUBI89). Electric shock as aversion therapy has no effect against amphetamine or cocaine use: the rush from a "good" injection of methamphetamine is more powerful than even a tetanic electric shock.

The difference between the mental state of the addict and the mental factors that might predispose a person to addiction may be one of quantity or quality. An addict is insane by virtually any definition: psychopathic, psychotic with paranoia, hallucinations, and delusions. The withdrawn teenager who has never used drugs but is fascinated by the gregarious speed freak is not a psychotic madwan. At least not yet.

The mental problems underlying addiction cannot be diagnosed by administering the MMPI to addicts in treatment centers. Suppose a speed freak injects methamphetamine for five days in a row, taking no food or sleep. When this addict "crashes," se experiences a low that only a prisoner of war might understand. After a year of abuse, would it not be likely se tests positive for bipolar disorder? Someone could argue that we are treating the addict in the present, not the past pre-addict, but the point is still valid. Recovering addicts (an addictive person not currently taking drugs) show no significant differences from the general population on MMPI scores.[10]

To narrow the focus, we can outline a few factors that are not the *cause* of addiction. (These factors, however, certainly could increase the probability that an individual might be addicted.)

Depression is not the common denominator: for many depressed people, it would simply be too much trouble to take drugs (PAPO87). Poor physical conditioning is not the answer: drug use is not uncom-

---

[10] Some studies show a slight 4-6 pattern typical of criminals (GEND70). The importance of this should not be exaggerated; incarcerated addicts are frequently used for such studies.

mon among athletes. Success is not the distinguishing factor: some people handle failure well, becoming addicts after they are successful. Physical disabilities, which certainly could cause isolation and low self esteem, do not predispose a person to addiction (MOOR90).

Nonprofessionals sometimes think drug users are stupid (another good example of mistaking the result for the cause). Three University of Arkansas students (who did not know each other initially), became addicted to methamphetamine and eventually became part of the famous Cummins/ Tucker prison system. All were Merit Finalists with IQs over 150. A fourth student with similar abilities, who played chess with one of the addicts but did not use drugs himself, finished his Bachelor's in three years and went to Berkeley law school.

Drug addicts often report sexual problems. An alcoholic is accused of exposing himself to young women; during recovery, he reports he never learned basic social skills such as asking a woman for a date. It is almost impossible to separate the cause from the effect: Did an underlying sexual problem "cause" addiction, or did the use of the chemical cause sexual misbehavior? The drug counselor sees an addict with problems, not a person with problems who might become an addict. Since we are concerned with predictability, the mental problems of one already addicted are of little value. It is, however, reasonable to assume that P_m is higher in any maladjusted individual.

Many addicts report feeling accepted for the first time by other drug users. The drug culture accepts interested newcomers for the psychological reason that the drug users are usually in violation of the law and justify their actions somewhat by accepting others who are also willing to violate the rules, and for the simple economic reason of having a market for their product. Drug users are happy (at least at first) due to the drug effects: this happiness translates into acceptance of others the user would not normally accept (SELZ80).

An addict, raised in a strong Catholic environment, reports that in spite of extreme guilt, se continued to masturbate as a teenager. Eventually, se felt powerless: se could do nothing to stop the masturbation, guilt or not.   His first exposure to alcohol, with a group of "supportive" high school friends, resulted in severe intoxication and an arrest.

Deprivation has similar effects. A child watched har mother bake and was given a mixing bowl so se could eat the remaining batter. Se asked for a little more uncooked cake batter. Har mother, tired of cooking and perhaps of life in general, replied, "You've had enough! Just wait until the cake's done like everyone else" in a tone that leaves little doubt. This incident – trivial compared with the deprivation we see in the inner city – was reported by an adult addict. Se stated, "As soon as I got away from my bitch mother, I make me a bowl of cake mix. I got sick trying to eat all of it." Imagine that a child of the Third World who has not eaten for several days is given a pipe full of opium. Would se willingly stop the drug escape just to return to starvation?

We have eliminated a number of psychological factors as a single, common denominator in drug addiction. Is there such a common mental factor? A graduating psychology student, asked by a freshman to define neurosis, replied, "Neurosis is being unhappy with the way you are." This definition is a good start. For predicting addiction, the question is not "Are you gay?" but "Are you unhappy with your sexual orientation?" (whatever it is). Simplistic "moral majority" psychology that defines a behavior as "against God's law" is of about as much help in halting addiction as a good hit of stuff (injection of heroin).

We cannot judge happiness or satisfaction by brief observation: the popular student body president, always at home in any crowd, may report feelings of loneliness. P_m could be as high for an individual for whom such reaction formation has become a dominant theme as it is for the shy, depressed individual.

Values for P_m can be assigned by considering certain mental dysfunction. All mental problems do not increase the probability of addiction: the raging nut who believes himself to be Napoleon or Jesus Christ would probably not touch any mood-altering drug, since their namesake (as traditionally portrayed) did not use drugs.

Obsessive-compulsive behavior	.05
Depression	.05
Perceived deprivation	.05

7. Assigning a Value to Factor P_m

Because it deals with the psychology of a single individual (rather than effects due to a crowd or the environment), factor P_m can perhaps be assigned as accurately as that for the drug itself (P_s). I believe a test or interview could be developed to accurately assess factor P_m. Verifying the predictive ability would be difficult, since the uncovering of a deep emotional problem may help alleviate it: as with the electron, the act of observation itself means the observed is no longer the same. Empirical evidence is difficult to obtain for another reason: Is it ethical to sit idly observing drug use in the high-risk group just to find out if any of them become addicts?

Environmental Factors (P_e)

This section deals with the environment the addict is seeking to escape, in contrast with factor P_p which deals with the environment of the drug subculture that attracts the would-be addict. Even a very bad environment does not cause addiction by itself; likewise, a very good environment does not guarantee immunity from addiction. The idea of using drugs solely for escape is too simplistic: many addicts report drinking or using other drugs to celebrate. Rather than escape the problem, they handle the problem and then take the drug as a reward.

Popular conceptions such as "Indians and alcohol don't mix" are occasionally backed up by statistics (LEND82). This, of course, could be genetic, but an alternate explanation is also possible. Imagine that your home is a vast land, rich in resources, which your people would never even consider abusing. A group invades, bringing powerful weapons and theories of how the land should be managed, kills most of your people and orders you to remain in an area a millionth the size of your original land. The invaders bring something called money. You must now do whatever small tasks the invaders allow so you can have enough of this paper to buy your food. The invaders are also willing to trade a powerful liquid that takes away all the pain of history for the money.

It is not possible to discuss an environment conducive to addiction without dealing with factors such as the European settler's destruction of the home of the American Indian (SUND70). This is not limited to a single group: the newest minority may be the Caucasian middle class! One middle class addict complained, "The Republicans represent big business and the rich and the Democrats represent the poor and everyone on welfare. Who represents ME?" For the purposes of addiction, it is the perception of unfairness that is important. If, however, a society is inequitable, more individuals are likely to have a perception of unfairness.

Are sociological factors simply an excuse? Although an addict will eagerly seize any excuse to consume drugs, a truly bad environment definitely increases the probability of addiction. Imagine a child whose family consists of an obese mother, four brothers, all of whom have done jail time, and two older sisters, both of whom have been arrested for prostitution. At first, she wants to complete high school and "make something of herself" (she is not sure what that is, but she is positive it is not the life she has seen so far). She tries to study at home amid the screaming family and occasional gunshots from down the block. Finally, in the tenth grade, she drops out of school.

She is introduced to crack cocaine: all her problems and disappointments melt after one inhalation from the pipe. (Remember that inhaled cocaine vapor reaches the brain in about 11 seconds.)

Several years later, our subject has a child, born severely premature, who cries constantly. The subject (and perhaps the child) has chronic lung and sinus trouble, a heart murmur, several diseases transmitted by sex or IV drug use (she is not sure which). She now wants to stop using cocaine. After enough trouble with the law, she is put into a good drug treatment program. The staff recommends at least six weeks, but Rule 24/25[11] funding only pays for 28 days. For one month, she eats better than she ever has. Her room is quiet, private, and safe. She has older people who really listen to her, and peers who talk to her for herself, not what they can get. She wants to be "well," "cured," "recovering," and she makes excellent progress.

After 28 days, with the fanfare that accompanies completion of treatment, she is released into her mother's custody. What is the probability she will remain drug-free?

Some environments are intolerable. No person *should* adapt to them: to do so would be just as insane as drug use. An addict creates har own world, and many never return from it. Sometimes, overdose, prison, or a lingering insanity from hallucinogens or inhalants may actually be preferable to the addict's real world. Environment includes not only the geography, but also the family and culture. Again, the perception of the addict is of prime importance.

(If we are trying to understand addiction, or to treat the addict, we must remember that addicts have highly developed social skills in one

---

[11] This law may be particular (peculiar?) to Minnesota. I am sure similar laws exist in other states of the United States, where funding is always limited except for military and CIA operations.

area: obtaining drugs and making excuses for their drug use. If we allow that a bad environment may be the "cause" of addiction, we give the addict from that environment carte blanche to use. The thesis of this book is that there is no single cause of addiction. As with other factors, a bad environment increases the probability of addiction and not even as much as other factors. Addicts seeking to recover must not be allowed to justify their drug use, even when it is justified!)

Factor P_e is found by summing all adverse environmental factors are summed to arrive at a value, not to exceed .25. Box 8 shows factors

Immediate, physical danger	.07
Long-term health threats	.07
Inadequately met basic needs	.07
Cannot achieve goals	.07

8. Assigning a Value to Factor P_e

suspected of contributing to P_e.

These are assigned in keeping with Maslow's hierarchy of needs (MASL54). If a child is constantly hungry, for example, se may not be as concerned as others about not being able to act in the school play. Modern cities have added a new peak to the hierarchy, immediately below the need for air: avoidance of imminent death. Immediate physical danger refers such things as "drive by" shootings or being beaten senseless by a drunk father.

Soldiers always face grotesque death from many sources. Clear battle lines as in World War II, however, allowed some perception of safety for those "behind front lines." With no such lines in the Vietnam War, the perception of danger was constant. The Vietnam War produced many addicts, and they often continued to use drugs after they came home. Perhaps some of the 2,600 Unites States POWs and MIAs have wasted away in the opium dens of the East, and looking for their remains on the battlefields is useless.

Long-term health threats include constant noise, air pollution, and overcrowding. Overcrowding also increases the probability of drug use; studies show that animals in crowded environments voluntarily choose water containing amphetamines over plain water (SCIN85). With a reasonable allotment of space, animals avoid the bitter amphetamine solution (unless they are already addicted).

The addict is usually unaware of the specifics of the environment, but when pressed se will report the problem with a generality such as "This city SUCKS." Long-term health threats are rated the same as immediate danger because they represent a constant annoyance and thus a reason to want to escape.

"Dangers" are factors that should not be present, but are; inadequate basic needs are those factors that should be present but are not. The perception of adequacy for food, shelter, and clothing varies greatly: if a child perceives expensive tennis shoes as vital, cheaper ones are seen as inadequate and embarrassing. Such perceptions are pathological (no one really needs designer jeans): the twisted perception probably results from a genuine earlier neglect or may be indicative of serious mental disfunction. Whatever the cause, a teenager's perception of him/herself as disadvantaged compared to peers increases the probability of escape behavior.

The inability to achieve goals can be seen in reverse: by dealing with recovery. An executive in a high-pressure advertising firm undergoes treatment for alcohol and Valium addiction. Se returns to a supportive family, an upper-class neighborhood, and coworkers determined to absorb some of the pressure. How are har chances compared to those of our poor, uneducated ghetto dweller? If the would-be addict (or recovering addict) sees no chance for change and no chance for ever achieving har goals, the immediate gratification world of drugs gains attractiveness. The probability of addiction, in the form of factor P_e, increases.

P_e also helps explain the inadequacy of imprisoning addicts and much of the ineffectiveness of the penal system in general. Even if life was not misery for the potential addict, it certainly was misery by the last stage of addiction. How does the judicial system expect to threaten a person with three decent meals per day, a quiet existence, and an environment that is actually safer than their home?

The downright fascist "mandatory sentencing guidelines" that imprison a kid for ten years for mailing two LSD tablets to a friend do not solve the problem either.

Psychological Addiction

Traditionally, psychological addiction would properly be covered in this chapter because it has always been considered a characteristic of The Individual, not the chemical substance. Drug addiction is now considered a disease, even by the conservative American Medical Association. This was not always the case: the town drunk was a classic object of ridicule and abuse since medieval times. Psychological addiction, in contrast, is still looked upon as some sort of weakness of will.

Let me repeat a paragraph from Chapter 1: Before 1980, everyone (except the addicts) maintained that heroin was "truly" addicting while cocaine was only "psychologically" addicting. In the 1980's, the lay press, opposing current scientific thought, labeled "crack" the most addicting substance known. What really are the differences between heroin addiction and cocaine addiction? Addicts became liars, thieves, and prostitutes for either drug. Abrupt withdrawal of either drug following months of continuous use caused pain sufficient to keep the addict acting in ways undesirable even to the addict.

What is psychological addiction? Someone who thinks se is addicted to something? Would that person lie, cheat, or prostitute themselves to obtain the drugs? As William James said, "A difference that makes no difference is no difference."

I believe the term psychological dependence has no value in the realm of chemical addiction. The term simply indicates the ignorance of science in not yet locating the exact mechanism – the chemical in the body that is being replaced.   You may have shared the experience of feeling absolutely terrible for no reason you could fathom and have a colleague state "it's just a virus." This is a safe diagnosis, since viruses are small and difficult to eliminate as a cause. Psychological addiction may be the mental equivalent of the ubiquitous virus.

If psychological addiction has any meaning, it is being addicted to a lifestyle. Hangin' with friends. Making it to the dope man's house just in time to cop (obtain some drugs) for the night.   In my version of psychological addiction, the would-be addict cannot actually obtain enough drugs of sufficient purity to alter the body's chemistry on any long-term basis (a condition required for addiction).

A woman who had drank alcohol heavily and accompanied it with barbiturates remained drug free for several years and then reported being addicted to Midol™. She had been arrested for shoplifting: stealing half a dozen packages of Midol. Former addicts report being addicted to aspirin or ibuprofen. Psychological addiction, in the sense of being addicted to something that is not addicting, has traditionally been looked at as the reason for her behavior.

Perhaps psychological addiction is just a very high propensity for becoming addicted (P_i). Whatever the case (if there even is one), drugs are not psychologically addicting. Either they are addicting , as per Axiom 1, or they are not. People, however, are much more complicated: they can claim to be whatever they desire.

Chapter 3
Implications

Drug addiction has two components: the chemical substance (Chapter 1) and the characteristics of the individual (Chapter 2). Assuming the first two chapters describe a reasonably accurate model of drug addiction, it is possible to predict when an addiction will occur.

If we can say a person will most likely become a drug addict, is that person responsible? Should we just put har in jail or treatment right now, before se ever even takes the first hit? Is this legal? After the individual becomes an addict, se does some things society would prefer to have undone. Is the addict responsible?

Consider methadone programs. Often, the addict arrives early, drinks the "cherry cough syrup" containing the methadone, and then spends all afternoon as a thief or prostitute getting money for more drugs. Not quite the success the government planned.

This chapter discusses the relevance of the probability model to the legal, medical, and social problems resulting from drug addiction. Before we do so, however, one important point should be made. This book presents a theory of probability that the disease of drug addiction will occur in a given individual, given certain conditions. A *probability*, not a certainty. We cannot say someone <u>will</u> become a drug addict.

And however unlikely the odds, we cannot say a given individual cannot get off drugs. *There is always a probability, for any drug addict, that se will stop using addicting chemicals.* By the probability theory as I have outlined it, no one is hopeless.

Legalization of
Controlled Substances

"Legalizing all controlled substances will cut down on crime."

The above simplification is espoused today by various members of the entire political spectrum. On one extreme are those simply desiring to get high in peace (without government interference). On the other end are conservatives who (presumably) do not go home and smoke a joint each evening: they simply feel that drug legalization would cut down on crime.

By roughly the same logic as that of the conservatives, we could avoid bank robberies and embezzlement by giving the perpetrators a card saying ROBBER or EMBEZZLER. This card lets the owner withdraw any amount of money from any automatic teller machine. We might also reduce overcrowding at prisons by allowing inmates to murder one another.

Actually, it is not so much the legalization of the drugs that would cause the problem. It is the alacrity with which capitalistic drug companies would jump on the chance to supply the drug. Within months, substances which were capable of causing addiction would proliferate. Increasing the availability of an addicting substance increases the probability that more people would try it. Some of these people have a high P_i rating; the probability is they would become addicted.

Prohibition: A Case Study

The United States once conducted a massive social experiment in the legalization of an addicting substance. In 1919, Article [XVIII] of the U. S. Constitution outlawed (within one year) the manufacture, importation, or exportation of alcoholic beverages. (Citizens were left to ponder how one might export something that could not manufacture.) In 1933, Article [XXI] repealed Article [XVIII], effectively legalizing the manufacture and sale of beverages containing the addicting chemical ethyl alcohol.

The 1920's became known as "prohibition" in the United States. Many fine books cover prohibition, a time of rampant disregard of the law, the rise of Chicago's powerful mobs, and "speak-easys" where even the authorities knew that alcoholic drinks were always available. Because the manufacture of ethyl alcohol was illegal, its quality was not monitored, and "bathtub gin" sometimes contained an additional fermentation product: methanol. This alcohol kills in sufficient quantity, but destroys the optic nerve in almost any concentration.

Present-day advocates of drug legalization cite the flagrant disregard of laws and the poor quality of the non-commercial product, pointing to prohibition as an example. Certainly, some comparisons are valid. But did the repeal of prohibition in 1933 lessen *the number of alcoholics in society?* And did Article [XXI] in the long run help society?

Margaret Mead once said that a visitor from another world might well think automobiles were the dominant life form.[12] In the 1920's, this was not the case, making a comparison of drunk driving statistics worthless. Today, the combination of alcohol and automobiles kills more effectively than most weapons developed specifically for the purpose. It is legal for an individual to stop at numerous places of camaraderie, inject a limited quantity of a powerful, addicting drug, and return to sailing two tons of metal at a tenth the speed of sound between two painted lines (while a lot of others are attempting the same feat).

The importation, manufacture, and sale of beverages containing ethyl alcohol has made a number of people comfortably wealthy. Because of the respect this garners in our society, we are not likely to see "prohibition" again in the near future. But is our society better off? Would driving with an acceptable blood level of cocaine really benefit us all?

Heroin is certainly as effective as alcohol in impairing a person's ability to operate a motor vehicle, yet we do not see the carnage due to use of heroin. It is not because heroin use is not as macho as alcohol

---

12 And this was twenty years ago! Traffic has probably not decreased, so we can safely use the great anthropologist's quote in the 1990's.

use: visit a biker's bar and ask. It is not due to the fact that junkies who have cars can seldom find them: alcoholics lose entire automobiles also. The reason we do not see war-like death totals due to an automobile-heroin mix is that heroin is not legal. The use of heroin is not as widespread. Heroin is more expensive.

Perhaps the repeal of prohibition lessened organized crime (or made it better organized and legal?), but did the legalization of alcohol lessen the number of alcoholics? I have not researched this question, but, given the model this book presents, I would bet that the percentage of alcoholics in the population rose. In certain areas – Indian reservations, for example[13] – where alcohol was scarce, the repeal of probition virtually destroyed the society (SUND70, anecdotal).

Logistics Problems

When viewed as an intellectual discussion, legalizing all controlled substances may seem as good an idea as the Vietnam War did to Eisenhower. The logistics, however, make the Tet Offensive seem rudimentary. How much of the drug is an individual allowed to purchase? All se wants? Suppose we limit the amount of the drug any one person can buy. (Do we allow additional purchases for the invalid mother?) Would anyone, having read this text (or not!), seriously think the addict would take the amount of a drug allowed by a semi-

---

[13] The American Indians were once a people as noble in reality as the Klingons are in fiction. Confinement to "reservations" certainly increased P_e for these people. The white man, always alert for a profit, was right at the door with "fire water." The enormous success of Casinos in present times is again prompting the "paleface" to try to live off the Indians' success in the form of taxes.

conscious government bureaucrat and then go happily home to watch reruns of *The Partridge Family*?

If we give the addict unlimited access to har drug of choice, we might as well just shoot the addict (with a bullet). If we limit the amount of the drug we are making available, then the legalization fails in its goal of reducing crime. The addicts still require an additional (illegal) supply,

The next logistics problem is Who pays for the drug? After we add the taxes necessary to feed the colony of bureaucratic microbes any government program generates and factor in corporate profit, the drugs cost more than they did on the streets. How many taxpayers want to give "worthless dope fiends" all the drugs they want? If the drug supply is not free, however, the prostitution and thievery will remain just as necessary as before the legalization. (Addicts are not famous for their Clifford Trusts, IRAs, and judicious use of savings accounts.)

Table 3. Logistics Problems in Legalizing Controlled Substances

• How much can be purchased?
• Who pays for it?
• Will it be available NOW?

Even a non-addict who has read this book must appreciate the power of the more addicting drugs. Exposure to an addicting substance is a factor in the probability of addiction. Increasing availability will increase exposure: kids using the parents' supply, addicts sharing their "good fortune" with those not yet addicted, the curious with a high addiction potential (P_i). Whatever else (if anything) the legalization of addicting drugs might accomplish, it is highly probable it will increase the number of addicts.

The most powerful reason for not making drugs readily available is not easy to understand by non-addicts. We could call it "addict's time." The addict needs the drug right now. Not after a Congressional debate. Not when the drug store opens. Not when it is convenient for a bitchy nurse to hand it out. NOW! If there are packages of cocaine on the shelf in the drug store, a Stage 3 addict is not likely to loiter around waiting for opening time. Of course, addicts could buy their supply ahead of time. Of course they would not use it up. Of course, no one else would steal their supply.

In fairness, most of the argument presented in this section is from logistics: the difficulty in implementing the legalization of drugs whose distribution and use is currently controlled by the government. Logistics is never a complete argument. Certainly, the logistics of having a person walk on the moon were formidable.

The second part of the argument against legalization is consequences. Legalization of highly addicting drugs in a capitalist system means someone would soon find a way to profit from making these substances readily available. The availability increases the likelihood that a vulnerable individual (high P_i) would be exposed to an addicting substance. The probability of addiction theory predicts that increasing the availability of addicting substances would increase the number of addicts in society. The chances that legalizing addicting drugs would ultimately help society is about the same as the probability that the Catholic Church will open a chain of abortion clinics.

Decriminalization

I have argued that the legalization of currently controlled substances would increase the availability of the addicting drugs, leading to increased exposure, and an increase in the number of drug addicts. I have also commented on the dubious benefits of sentencing a 17-year-old to ten years in prison for mailing two tablets of LSD to his friend. How can I resolve the dilemma that drugs must be either legal or illegal?

A middle choice in handling the legal status of currently controlled substances is "decriminialization" (BUCK73). I am defining decriminalization of controlled substances as the elimination of most penalties for the possession of the drug. The production and sale of the addicting drug is not legal, but the possession of the drug is not a criminal offense, or at most a minor offense. After 50 years of research, medical and psychological thinking began seeing drug addiction as a disease. As soon as the pronouncement was made, the United States legal system began treating addiction as immoral behavior!

Previous arguments against the legalization of controlled substances were based on the damage it would likely do to society. As a free people, we do not put the needs of society ahead of the individual. The state, the theory goes, is there to protect the individual and to ensure "life, liberty, and the pursuit of happiness" (HANC76). Drug legalization would probably not be good for the individual, but neither is a prison cell.

If drug use is not (completely) criminal and drug users are not (completely) in control of their actions, should addicts be held (completely) accountable for other crimes they commit? How does the judge and legislator deal with the taunt they are "soft on crime"? What do we do with someone who simply will not quit using drugs and committing other criminal acts to support har habit?

If we do not ever plan to modify society so that it can provide a sane environment for all our citizens, we might as well feed drugs to the "less fortunate" and let them die in peace.

Treatment of Chemical Addiction

Professionals who deal with addicts are acutely aware that many things do not stop drug addiction. The best-intentioned addict/alcoholic returns to using the chemical substance, sometimes after years of abstinence. This section examines the problems of treating addicts, some fruitless or outright dangerous "treatments," and some actions that can help. Using the probability concept defined in this book, we can see that many treatments do not decrease the probability of

- **Blind Sympathy**.

  The addict will use any means necessary to obtain drugs, including your kindness or good will.

- **Blind Justice: Punishment**

  Compared to what an inner-city junkie endures, daily, prison is a safe, comfortable, healthy environment.

- **Giving Drugs**

  Tautological: This seems so obvious that it is inane to even list it. Yet the U.S. Government

9. Actions Not Likely to Help Drug Addiction

addiction and some may increase it. While we cannot permanently cure drug addiction (not at this time, anyway), we can decrease its probability.

Ineffective Treatments

The probability concept (or common sense, for that matter) should point out the difficulties of treating drug addiction by giving addicts drugs. Making the more powerful chemicals widely available also is an unneeded danger to society. Methadone programs operate under the faulty assumption that giving drugs to an addict satisfies her or him. This is like thinking parallel lines meet somewhere and rushing off at high speed down the highway to find that point. Axiom 3 corrects this faulty geometry.

Axiom 3

An addiction cannot be satisfied. Feeding it will only make it larger.

When an addict has reached Stage 3, a pattern has been engraved in har mind that cannot be erased. The addict has also learned a lifestyle that met many of har needs, even if it did so by masking reality. Close association with the lifestyle is likely to lead the addict to return to active addiction. Similarly, use of a mood-altering drug, even in a different setting, is likely to return the addict to the lifestyle.

Methadone programs attempt to cure addiction by providing an addicting drug (cf: former President Reagan's "Peacekeeper" missile). Addicts will stick many holes in their arms with a safety pin or inject cold water or Epsom salts just to have "tracks" so they can get on a methadone program. The addicts go in the morning to pick up a dose of methadone and then search the streets all afternoon for other drugs. Sometimes, they trade the "take-home" methadone–given for days the clinic is closed–for stimulants. They also attempt to inject this oral methadone, in spite of various syrupy additives designed to prevent this.

1. Controlled, oral dispensation of a pure drug in a clinical setting is better than use of IV street drugs.

2. Methadone does not damage the immune system; heroin does.

3. Although the withdrawal from methadone lasts longer than that from heroin, it is not as severe.

10.   Justifications for Methadone Programs

Point 1 ignores the power and desperation of addiction. Addicts will inject methadone mixed with cherry cough syrup. They may even inject the cherry cough syrup without methadone! Point 2 is probably not true: one addict bragged of "cutting" heroin with "baby laxative." Supposedly injectable street drugs contain dust, dirt, talcum powder, cleanser, and even drain cleaner. Street "junk" is sometimes just that: it may be less than 1 percent heroin (POLI79). Injecting the adulterating agents damages the immune system; there is no evidence to my knowledge that pure heroin does such damage (lowering of PMNs/sedimentation rate, for example).

Point 3 is spurious: most withdrawals last much longer than generally supposed and addicts often do not fear it anyway, except to the extent that such fear excuses further drug use. (The withdrawal symptoms from abruptly stopping 70 to 80 milligrams of methadone per day are significantly worse than those from all but the purest heroin.)

Axiom 4

If substance A is addicting and substance B can replace substance A, then substance B is also addicting.

Corollary

Drug addiction cannot be effectively treated with a mood-altering chemical.

The corollary explains why most addicts, at least in the first three years of recovery, smoke cigarettes and drink coffee. It also explains a strange behavior seen at Alcoholics Anonymous meetings: the alcoholics meet in evenings to consume large quantities of coffee and smoke cigarettes. Many Alcoholics Anonymous clubs consider it a duty and honor as part of Twelfth Step, to arrive early and make coffee for the group. Although coffee is not as dangerous as alcohol for the "average" person, it is addicting and mood altering. It is particularly likely to produce addiction in a recovering alcoholic.

In non-addicts, coffee may contribute to mood swings, depression, and irritability. The mood of the addict, however, is not so much altered as maintained. Their mood is altered–for the worse–when the substance is not available. (See Axiom 2.)

As mentioned, psychotherapy alone is ineffective against (active) drug addiction. Suppose a junkie has a copy of the A1 gene from both parents (and suppose this is meaningful ...), lives with alcoholic parents in an inner-city slum, has a tenth-grade education, and has been injecting heroin for five years. For this individual, we can make the calculations for the likelihood this person will become addicted to *something* (P_i).   We can also calculate the probability that a given chemical substance produces addiction (P_c).   We combine these to get the probability that the individual will become addicted to the chemical:

$$P_i := .30 + .25 + .25 \qquad\qquad \text{(maximum .50)}$$
$$= .50$$

$$P_c := .30 + .10 + .25 \qquad\qquad \text{(maximum .50)}$$
$$= .50$$

and then combine these two into a probability this individual will become addicted to this chemical as

$$P_a := P_s + P_i$$
$$= 1.0$$

Under the conditions given, our subject will become addicted.   A successful psychoanalysis which virtually eliminated underlying depression, isolation, and resentment against parents, could reduce P_m from .25 to .00.   (Zero means no contribution toward the likelihood of addiction due to this factor.)   This, however, would barely affect the total probability of addiction P_a, since factor P_i would still reach its maximum.

The probability of treating addiction successfully is low anyway; in an unwilling subject, it is virtually zero.   Treatment centers have only a limited time to fix a problem that has taken years to develop.   In a sincere desire to earn the large sums paid them by distraught parents and insurance carriers, they use a variety of techniques convince all patients they are addicts. Clients probably are at least in Stage 1 of addiction, with many in Stage 2. At these stages, however, most addicts are simply not sufficiently damaged by their drug use to want to quit. At this point in their addiction, their chances of remaining drug free for any substantial time are low.

Perhaps there is a point in addiction where the pain of quitting is overshadowed by the pain and difficulties of continuing. This is called "hitting bottom" by recovering alcoholics. The chronic addict eventually wants get out of the addiction cycle, but genuinely cannot imagine a life without drugs. Sometimes the addict stops on har own initiative and goes through the torture of withdrawal, only to begin using again. This return to drug use is because the basic factors contributing to the probability of addiction have not changed. This is perhaps the origin of the term "dry drunk": a former addict with behaviors usually associated with active addiction. P_i is high for this person.

Treating Medical Problems in Drug Addicts

It is often not possible to separate earlier physical and mental problems that increased the probability of addiction from problems that resulted from the addiction itself. Whatever the source, some mental and physical problems of addicts require attention.[14] The first and most

---

[14] If the cancer eventually goes into remission. If the person dies of cancer, it makes little difference if se is a drug addict. Medical staff causes unnecessary suffering by withholding any narcotic, even the illegal heroin, from a terminal patient.

obvious is malnutrition: one user of phenmetrazine did not eat or drink anything for five days. William Burroughs' junkie whose bowels had not moved for three months would require medical attention (BURR59). Often, the addict responds quickly to well-balanced meals and vitamin supplements. An addict will sometimes stop using for a week to get healthier just so se can experience the drug effects more fully!

Even if all factors for an individual are low, there is approximately a 50:50 chance se will become addicted from heavy doses of a powerful narcotic for an extended time. After treatment of severe burns, prolonged pain such as that of the diabetic described in section 2, or cancer, the care provider might consider a drug treatment program for the patient.[15]

Treating pain in an addict is comparable to working on the bomb squad, except that the medical professional is playing with someone else's life instead of har own. As an example, we calculate the addiction potential of morphine injected intramuscularly as

$$P_s := P_c + P_a$$
$$= .30 + .06$$
$$= .36.$$

All pain is, of course, "in our heads," since our brain is the organ that interprets the sensations. We consider "real" pain to be the perception in the cerebral cortex of damage to enervated tissue; when

---

[15] If the cancer eventually goes into remission, the patient can be treated for drug addiction. If the person dies of cancer, it makes little difference if se is also a drug addict! Medical staff cause unnecessary suffering by withholding any narcotic from a terminal patient. (Heroin should be legalized for this use.)

no such damage can be found, we consider the pain psychosomatic. An injection of Xylocaine close to an afferent nerve blocks the electro-chemical pulse through the nerve: the tissue "below" the nerve block can be severely damaged, but there is no pain. The point is that pain cannot be defined by the damage body tissue has suffered (in spite of the protestations of insurance companies).

An addict is the opposite of the shaman who can walk on 1200° coals or the athlete who completes a gymnastic exercise in spite of a broken leg. Withdrawing from heroin (or methadone), the junkie can be burned walking into a sauna that would be enjoyable for a "normal" person. The pain for the addict is very real. With endorphin produc-tion atrophied, the addict may feel disabling pain because of something that would not normally "hurt." Addicts deal with the pain by taking more drugs. They are not misrepresenting the pain (at least not always): they may be genuinely convinced they are in some way "damaged" or different from "normal."

Treating depression in the addict is equally difficult. It is a physio-logical and psychological juggling act to find a drug that does not do more harm than good in a normal ($P_i < .10$) individual. In an addict, this act is performed on very thin 100-meter high tightrope with no net. Substances that change mood in a short time should never be used. These include diazepam (Valium), chlordiazepoxide (Librium), the phenothiazines (such as chlorpromazine/Thorazine). If chemical treatment is required, use lithium carbonate, a tricyclic antidepressant, fluoxetine (Prozac), or something else that works over a longer time. Don't ask the addict what se needs or has used in the past: an addict's built-in radar for selecting addicting chemicals is uncanny.

Recovering addicts remain in constant danger from exposure to mood-altering substances. Axiom 4 contains an important warning for all health care workers treating recovering addicts: avoid use of drugs whenever possible. The addict would have medical staff believe se is dying of some acute pain with a logical source such as a car wreck of years ago. Most of the pain experienced by an addict is the direct result of addiction. Every addict believes se is the exception to this rule: har pain is real; se really does need the drug. Physical pain is a superb reason for taking drugs. I have heard award-winning excuses such as smoking marijuana to control multiple sclerosis (not the associated pain, but the disease itself) and daily drinking to the point of liver damage because of bad teeth.

I do not advocate cruelty. Librium or Valium should be used for perhaps a week after stopping use of a powerful drug. (There is no withdrawal that requires a month of methadone.) Acute withdrawal can kill, directly or from suicide. Take care, however, when prescribing any mood-altering drug, including painkillers, antianxiety drugs, or even a decongestant, for an addict. Use the minimum necessary to prevent severe discomfort and end drug therapy as soon as possible.

When medically necessary, an addicting drug does not seem to have the same effect as when taken "for fun." Recovering addicts who have been without any drugs for a long period report severe apprehension at the prospect of procedures such as surgery that might require use of narcotics. Although they do not always have trouble with limited, carefully-managed use of painkillers, the danger is still there. The recovering addict, exposed to narcotics in a medical setting, does not seem to remember a "high." This is consistent with the replacement model condensed in Axiom 1. During the trauma, the body needs more of the natural painkillers than it can produce. The foreign (addicting) agent does not replace endorphins, it augments them.

When are painkillers required? Obviously, first degree burns over 15 percent of the body requires morphine; a minor car wreck 10 years ago (with no damage showing on X-ray) does not. The addict's genius in obtaining drugs adds severe complications. One woman formerly addicted to narcotics had all her teeth pulled from her lower right jaw, one at a time, just so she could obtain meperidine from the oral surgeon. The health professional must attempt to separate the wheat from the chaff when listening to an addict and not blame herself or himself when the addict pulls one over on him. (Repercussions against the next addict seeking help may drive har to seek solace in the streets.)

If some drug is necessary to keep the addict from fleeing the treatment center, prescribe a substance with no CNS effects. Try a vitamin first: addicts love any pills and usually need vitamins anyway. Explain that it will make har feel much better. This would not be a lie. Any pill plus an authoritative explanation is likely to make a drug addict feel better.

Threats to Recovery

Recovering addicts often distinguish between two different situations that return them to drug use. A "slip" occurs when the former addict uses an addicting substance once or twice and stops. A "relapse" is when the former addict goes back into the lifestyle of continuous use after some period of being "clean" or "sober." (As with other terminology used by drug addicts, these definitions are not always fully separated.) Nonetheless, it is easy to distinguish these two conditions: the addict who has a slip is not terribly damaged physically and is penitent to the point of obsequiousness. The addict who has relapsed quickly looks as bad as before stopping use of the drug and may be quite defiant if challenged.

An addict taking a drug once is cause for worry, but it does not necessarily imply wholesale return to the addiction lifestyle. We want to consider factors that might lead the recovering addict to relapse: use of any mood-altering drug is an important factor. In addition, the recovering addict faces danger from suicide, retribution from former associates who feel wronged, and death from the physical ailments such as AIDS to which the addict may have been exposed.

The major danger to recovery, however, is the set of mental justifications that enables the addict to use the chemical substance and ignore the consequences: these can easily drive the addict back into active addiction.

Suicidal tendencies do not result as much from the pain of withdrawal as from the realization, as the addict says, "that I screwed up my entire life." Even for the most devoted drug user who has lost family, friends, and a job, this is an exaggeration. But true or not, it is dangerous way to think. In an addict just off drugs, this is probably not "underlying depression." It is an entirely logical reaction to the damage the addict has caused and endured, augmented by unbalanced neurotransmitters. Excellent therapy is contact with other recovering addicts, in a treatment or support group. The addict feels very isolated; realizing that others have the same feelings has remarkable salutary effects.

Peer pressure is possibly a bigger factor in remaining drug free than it was in taking drugs in the first place. In advanced stages, the addict has few acquaintances not directly involved in the use or trading of drugs. The addict is told by a counselor or parole officer to avoid har old buddies. Okay, who does the former addict talk to? The former addict's loneliness is augmented by drug withdrawal and severe feelings of "having ruined my whole life."

The pressure from former associates will probably be in the nature of a ribbing, "Oh? You quit again this month, huh? Let's go have a drink and talk about it." It can be much worse. Threats are sometimes made for money allegedly owed and the former addict's associate mentions how se could pay off the debt by "doing one more deal." An addict who once manufactured amphetamines for a small syndicate was asked to "make just one more batch" after he had stopped using the substance himself. He politely and sincerely explained to his syndicate contact – who had seen abscesses on his arms – that the drug was killing him and he had to avoid all contact with it. He agreed to pay them a small amount for equipment they had purchased for him. In spite of the popular idea that no one can ever leave "the mob," no retribution occurred.

Physical effects of addiction might include acquired immune deficiency syndrome, cirrhosis, and chronic hepatitis. The effects are certain to include malnutrition, poor dental hygiene, and general physical malaise. This book is not primarily about medical treatment (except where it inadvertently aids addiction), but the physical results of addiction must not be ignored. Treatment programs should provide vitamin supplements and refer clients to proper medical services. Chiropractic care may be excellent for recovering addicts because it seems to alleviate number of general aches and pains for which there are no clear physical ailments. The addict must not be allowed excuses for continuing drug use. As one counselor was fond of saying, "The best excuses are the real ones."

While the former addict no longer needs their drug of choice to function (according to Axiom 3), the thinking persists long after effective withdrawal from the drug. Such thinking can easily become a self-fulfilling prophesy. Quitting the drug and removing herself or himself from the drug environment, the recovering addict no longer has the usual coping mechanisms and may become severely depressed. Since se knows there are antidepressant drugs, the addict naturally thinks these are the solution. (Modern antidepressants that act to restore normal chemical functioning in the brain may be a partial answer.) Do not give mood-altering drugs such as diazepam to a former addict!

The effects of some drugs injected intravenously (IV) are so powerful that no other experience is comparable. A similar effect is achieved, but with more consistent effort, by persistent use of a less-addicting (lower P_s) drug such as marijuana or alcohol. The drug gave the addict support, comfort, and sometimes even substituted for food and sleep. After injecting phenmetrazine, some addicts would not breathe for several minutes; speed freaks sometimes do not eat or drink anything for almost a week. Selling the drug (dealing) presents a livelihood, with promises of instant riches, for the addict. In talking with hundreds of addicts, however, I have never seen even one become rich by selling drugs.

Part of the relapse problem, frustrating psychologists and treatment counselors for years, is that withdrawal probably lasts a lot longer than current medical texts allow: the EEG, for example, will not return to normal for eight months following a single injection of heroin (SCIN85). It seems to the therapist that the addict waits until the worst of the pain is over and then uses again! Acute pain from withdrawal may last from weeks to months, but it may take years to restore normal brain function. A newcomer to Alcoholics Anonymous complained at a meeting, "God, I've been sober for a month and I still feel bad." A more-experienced member with years of sobriety laughed heartily and replied, "Hell, it'll be six months before you even feel human."

Active use of the drug hides the real mess the addict has made of har life. This quasi-real state gradually ends after drug use stops and the addict, perhaps never well adapted to reality to begin with, sees only a world of emptiness and terror. Staying clean and sober just does not seem worth it. Suicide is all too common at this point.

A recovering addict often experiences symptoms similar to those of posttraumatic stress syndrome for years after stopping drug use. Addicts frequently report dreaming they took a drink or injected a drug. They awake with rapid heartbeat and pulse, wet with sweat, unable to tell they have not used the drug. Many report extreme guilt at having "used" again. The drug effects are so powerful that the experience simply cannot be erased from memory. The popular phrase "once an addict, always an addict" is stated alternatively by Axiom 5.

Axiom 5

A person who has ever been severely addicted to a chemical substance has a probability of addiction (P_1) starting at .50.

Corollary

A former addict can never safely use any mood-altering substance.

The science jury is still deciding if there is a genetic basis for addiction. Whether or not addiction is "natural" for some people, by Stage III, it has become an integral part of the addict. The drug addict has been permanently altered to be extremely susceptible to the effects of all mood-altering chemicals. Narcotics Anonymous warns that "Thinking of alcohol as different from other drugs has caused a great many addicts to relapse" (NAWS87). Some Alcoholics Anonymous members who "wouldn't touch a drop" became addicted to marijuana because they felt it was not as "bad for them" as was alcohol. The alcoholic often thinks marijuana is not really "addicting," underlining the futility and danger of separating physical and psychological addiction.

Axiom 5 hints at another danger to recovery: after some period without drugs, the addict may think se is cured. Although no reputable treatment center would claim to "cure" addicts, the person frequently does emerge from treatment feeling "in control," due to the combination of a structured environment, regular therapy, good nutrition, and (usually!) abstinence from drugs and alcohol. This is a dangerous state of mind and many treatment programs offer "relapse prevention" which serves to "scare the addict a little." A recovering addict must act as if anything relating to drugs (including alcohol) is an uninsulated power line: it's not impossible to touch it, but you'd better be prepared and very careful.

This point deserves stressing: the former addict must become almost fanatic about avoiding all addicting substances. When se refuses fruit cake because it contains brandy or declines to take codeine after removal of three wisdom teeth, the addict is being careful, not fanatical. Things such as "near beer" may be dangerous to recovering alcoholics, who are already heavily conditioned to deal with all problems by ingesting alcohol. Although P_s is less for the low-alcohol drink, P_i starts at .50 in the former addict. The chances of the former addict becoming addicted to any mood-altering chemical (and perhaps many other less than desirable behavior) are not zero. They are better than 50:50.

The third danger is what the addicts call "slippery places," the environment in which the addict took drugs. This is the physical and mental environment: it is the building, crack house, or country club, but it is also the associates and the mental state of the drug user. Treatment centers warn of the danger of such mental states with the HALT rule: Never get too Hungry, Angry, Lonely, or Tired. In the context of probability, it is not *impossible* for an alcoholic to frequent a bar and remain sober, but har chances of winning the lottery are probably better. Assuming at least five happy patrons in the bar, some of whom may be "old drinking buddies," we can calculate a value for Pa as shown in the box. This former alcoholic has a 95 percent chance of going back to active addiction. Stated another way, with har present activities, se has only a 5 percent chance of remaining sober.

$$P_i = .50 \text{ (Axiom 5)}$$

$$P_p = .25 \text{ (assuming five happy patrons)}$$

$$P_a := .50 + .25$$
$$= .85$$

11.   Sample P_a Calculation for a Former Addict

If the addict has not fully dealt with mental, financial, and emotional problems, P_m also contributes another .20, yielding a probability of 1.00 (maximum) that addiction will occur. Axiom 5 states that P_i begins at .50, not that it is .50. Although psychological problems are included in the equation for P_i, they are still added to the .50 value. We can look

at the .50 as something like a state-dependent reinforcement factor, making the recovering addict a superb candidate for addiction if exposed to any mood-altering drug. Previous addiction adds greatly to the chances of future addiction. Table 4 summarizes dangers to a former addict earnestly trying to remain drug free.

Table 4. Dangers to Recovery

Using A Different Addicting Substance

- "My problem was alcohol. Smoking dope never did   cause me any trouble. Why should it now?"
- "It's only beer. It's not like I'm drinking whiskey."
- "Pills won't hurt me. At least I'm not shooting anything."

Pressure from Former Associates

- "You WHAT? Hell, you quit twice already this month!"
- "What's the matter? Wife on your case again?"
- "Hey, this stuff is GOOD. You can quit again tomorrow."
- "Oh, take a Valium. Se won't seem like such a jerk then."

Idea that Drugs are Necessary

- "I'm different. My body *needs* the drug."
- "My teeth are bad; alcohol kills the pain."
- "I need it to stay awake at work (asleep at night)."

Feeling Cured

- "I can take a drink now and then without getting pickled."
- "So there's coke at the party. I don't have to use it."
- "I'm just going to the bar. I'm not going to drink."

Lowering The Probability
of Drug Addiction

What must we do to address addiction on a large scale? Part of the answer may surprise government officials: we are doing some things right already. If we slow the supply of drugs, we decrease the likelihood that an individual will be exposed to an addicting substance. Law enforcement helps lower the probability of addiction, except when they do stupid things like break into the wrong house or bully semi-conscious addicts into admitting their terrible crimes.[16] Making the "straight world" hostile to the addict does not lower the chances se will return to using.

Though it helps some, the "DEA approach" is like trying to screw the cap back on the fire hose after it has been turned on. A much better solution is improving the living standards of Colombians and Peruvians who grow coca and Asians who process raw opium into heroin. Herein lies the dilemma: an official of a capitalist government arrives in a black limosine with police escort to a small mountain village, explaining how his country can set up a factory to pay the ignorant peasants 50 cents a day. "It will, however, take a few yearsto get everything set up." The "ignorant peasant" can make 50 American dollars delivering a bundle at midnight to a plane in the valley.

---

[16] Since there are so many crimes in the United States, it is not hard for the well-informed police officer to find something: lying to a police officer, conspiracy to commit burglary, possession of a chemical that might be used to manufacture a controlled substance, almost any sexual activity. Jails and prisons are big business.

Primary drug treatment– separating the addict from the addicting chemical – is generally available in "detox" centers. Detox centers are well supported: they get those nasty drug addicts off the streets. Detox centers are basically jail cells painted with brighter colors. The addict is confined for 72 hours (a typical statutorial period a citizen may be confined without consent). This type of confinement is emergency-room only: it must be followed up with a regular drug treatment. Here, we must not be "understanding" about drug use: if the addict uses drugs, se is taken out of school and returned to primary treatment.

Techniques such as former President Reagan's "Just say no!" campaign or those who claim addicts will be cured if they just accept Jesus into their hearts may work in a few cases. (The former in those who never started using; the latter in those prepared to ignore a world of injustice for a reward after death.) In general, however, we must lower both the availability of addicting drugs and the tendency of individuals to use them. Both must be done in a sensible, realistic fashion.

Table 5.   Lowering Probability of Addiction

Lower Availability of Addicting Substances
- Provide alternative crops for coca and poppy growers
- End the hypocrisy of legal nicotine
- Halt advertising of ethyl alcohol
- Community service work in poor areas for those caught selling   drugs

Lower Probability Individuals Become Addicts
- Realistic drug education programs (use former addicts)
- Improve inner cities
  - less noise and pollution
  - worthwhile employment & more of it
  - decent minimum wage ($9/hr. 1996 $'s) for everyone who works: no exclusions
  - confinement of those with contagious diseases
- End subsidized reproduction of inner-city residents (*real* welfare reform)

Lower P_i for Former Addicts
- Primary treatment: detox, hospital
- Drug-addiction treatment (to include physical problems)
- Ongoing support: 12-Step groups, aftercare
- Treatment of underlying problems
- Job training and placement
- (All suggestions in previous box)

Appendix A
Probability

This appendix explains several concepts necessary to understand the mathematics of probability as it relates to the definitions in this book. The presentation does not simply state theory, but interweaves the theory with the application. The sections cover definitions of probability, related ideas such as "independent events," addition of probabilities, and "probable" versus "absolute": Will an event with a high probability always occur?

In scientific work, a probability is always less than or equal to 1 and is usually expressed as a decimal. The popular expression "the odds (something) will happen are 50:50" translates mathematically to "the event has a probability of occurrence of .5." Although the casual bettor uses "50:50" the scientist could properly use P = .50 only if the data are accurate to two decimal places.[17] A probability of 1.0 means the event will always occur:. Ben Franklin might have written "The probabilities for taxation and death are each 1.0." A probability of 0 means the event will not occur (a genuine tax decrease, for example).

A good system for explaining probability is one or more tossed

---

[17] For a number greater than 9, a zero in the right-most place is significant (meaning it represents real data and is not just a placeholder) only if the number has a decimal point: for 10., the 0 is significant; for 10, it is not. Rightmost zeros after (to the right of) a decimal point are always significant, since placeholders are on the left.

coins. We assume the coin has a distinct "head" side and "tail" side and that it is flipped into the air and allowed to land without interference. Many think that if a coin is tossed nine times and lands heads up, the tenth time, tails is very likely because it is somehow overdue. Treating each toss of the same coin as tosses of separate coins helps clear up this common misconception. Assuming nothing is "funny" about the coin, the probability of tails is the same on the tenth toss: 50:50, or $P = .5$. As experts warn, "Probability has no memory."

For more complicated events (such as drug addiction) that cannot be put under strict laboratory control, the probability is never 1 or 0. The bettor's "50:50" is more often the case.

With this admittedly short introduction, we can start the mathematics. The probability of two independent events (defined in a later section) *both* occurring is the *product* (not the sum) of the probabilities of each event occurring separately. Using the notation P_a for the probability that event "a" will occur, we have

$$P_{a \text{ and } b} = P_a \times P_b$$

or "The probability that events a and b will occur together is the product of the probability that event a will occur times the probability event b will occur. ($P_{a \text{ and } b}$ is commonly written as P_{ab}, assuming the common algebraic notation that $AB = A \times B$.) Since probabilities are always less than one, the product of two probabilities will always be less than the probability of either event: $1/2 \times 1/2 = 1/4$.

Although the formulas may seem overwhelming for those not

mathematically inclined, the idea does make intuitive sense. Suppose Pat purchases a lottery ticket where har odds of winning one dollar are 1:3 (P = .333). If se purchases two tickets, har odds of winning one dollar go up, but har odds of winning one dollar on *both* of the two tickets is lower. It is a lot lower: 1/3 x 1/3 = 1/9. Only one out of nine times will both tickets win.

As another example, consider the popular multi-million-dollar lotteries, with numbers picked by a method such as capturing airborne, numbered, "Ping-Pong" balls that are as identical as possible. If there are 45 balls, the chances of selecting the "2" ball with are 1/45 (P = .02222). The odds of the next ball being a "3", however, are not 1/45: because one ball has been used, the odds are now 1/44 (P = .02273). The math still works, however: the probability of getting both the "2" ball and the "3" ball is 1/45 x 1/44, or 1/1980. Since someone must match five or six balls exactly, it is easy to see why the odds against winning are so high.

(Note that there is no validity to computer lottery programs that claim to analyze subtle "patterns" in past lottery draws. As far as physics and mechanics are concerned, the machinery that picks lottery winning numbers produces random numbers. There is no pattern, although there are coincidences completely in keeping with probability. The huwan mind, due to its vast neuronal interconnections and virtually infinite ability to make more, and perhaps to motivation when free money is involved, can find patterns in anything. This does not imply predictability.)

To combine probabilities in this way or as explained in the next section, the events must be independent. The second section following covers this important concept, as it relates to probability and to the ideas presented in this book.

Summing Probabilities

Under what conditions are probabilities added? For two independent events, the prediction of either is the sum of the independent events. Again using P_a for the probability that event "a" will occur, we have

$$P_{a\,or\,b} = P_a + P_b$$

read as The probability of either event "a" or event "b" is the sum of the probability of event "a" plus the probability of event "b." If we have two or more independent events, each with some probability of occurring (P not = 0), the probability of any one of them occurring is greater than any single probability.

Again, this is intuitively understandable. If Pat buys two tickets for a five dollar drawing. the odds of winning five dollars, that is, the chance of either ticket, but not both, winning, is twice that of winning with one ticket.

Before returning to probability theory, let me apply what was just covered to addiction. Clearly, if a person is stressed in a way as to make drug addiction more likely, two such stressors are even more likely to make the person become an addict. If P_s, P_i, and P_a are probabilities (as explained in Chapter 1), then

$$P_a = P_s + P_i \quad (???)$$

presents us a mathematical dilemma. If each "event" or situation in the potential addict's life adds to the probability that the person will become addicted to a drug, we are justified in adding. The mathematics, however, tells us we can only add probabilities when dealing with one *or* the other, but not both.

This could be resolved mathematically by saying that either P_i *or* P_s will make an addict, giving the correct formula $P_a = P_s + P_i$. This, however, is not empirically true! Whatever the power of the substance (P_s) to cause an addiction, a hypothetical person with no propensity toward addiction (P_i) would not become an addict.[18] We might say that $P_i=0$ implies $P_a=0$, implying *and*, not *or*.

Note that we are not asking what the probability is that P_s or P_i will occur. Mathematically, the formula

$$P_{si} = P_s + P_i$$

is correct, but it is not what we are asking. We are not seeking to give

---

18   At least not a "street addict" or a person fully absorbed in drug-seeking behavior. Of course, any person forcefully injected with pure heroin for six months would be "addicted" in the sense that their bodily processes would be altered. With no propensity to addiction, however, this person would voluntarily stop the drug, provided the pain of withdrawal was properly handled.

the probability one of the two events (an addicting drug or an addiction-prone individual) will occur somewhere in our society. What we are seeking to predict is the likelihood that *if* the two events occur together, what are the chances (probability) the person who uses the drug will become a drug addict. These are decidedly different concepts. We can avoid the mathematical conundrum by writing the formula as

$$P_a := P_s + P_i \quad \text{(Chapter 1)}$$

or by considering P_s and P_i as components of P_a, but not strictly as probabilities (more on this in the next section). We are not in mathematical trouble if we remember that the left side of the equation is the probability of a third event and not a combination of the two "events" on the right side of the "equation."

Independent Events

Looking at any explanation of probability in a mathematics text, we are plagued by the term independent events. Every word "probability" is qualified by it, as in "the probability of two independent events A and B ...." What qualifies events as "independent"?

In mathematics, this independence means the occurrence of one event does not depend in any way on the occurrence of the other event(s). At the dependent extreme, we could say that a flipped coin landing heads' side up is totally dependent on its landing tails' side down: if it lands heads up, it cannot possibly be tails up. Stated mathematically, if the probability of heads is 1, the probability of tails is zero. Two coins represent the perfect independent event. If one coin lands heads up, it implies absolutely nothing about the other coin.

Everyone except the most rabid mathematicians recognizes that pure mathematics has little to do with reality. No complicated event in the real world is truly independent of every other event. Meteorology speaks of the Butterfly Effect: a butterfly flapping its wings in New York eventually results in a thunderstorm in China. (In 1993, we saw flooding in Iowa from the eruption of Pinatubo in the Philippines, making the Butterfly Effect seem less far fetched.) We now examine the mathematical idea of independent events as it relates to the all-too-real problem of drug addiction.

As an example, I imply that the factor that assesses mental/psychological problems (P_m) is independent of the environment factor (P_e) when these factors are summed in the "equation"

$$P_i := P_g + P_m + P_e \qquad \text{(Chapter 2).}$$

Of course, these factors are far from independent. Someone would have to be completely autistic to not be affected by their environment. We must assume independence among these factors for the sake of our model. Although statistical techniques exist for examining complicated, interrelated factors, this would add nothing to our model and would make it more difficult to use. (I have worked with 20-factor correlative FORTRAN programs with thousands of lines of code. Even when it worked, we learned little that was not obvious.)

Both the bad environment and the mental condition of the potential addict contribute to the probability of addiction. If factor P_m contributes .10, P_e contributes .10, we might give the contribution of the interaction of P_m and P_e as .05, and then decide whether to add or subtract .05 from the sum of Pm + P_e. The combination of these three values gives us no more information than simply modifying the values for both P_m and P_e to allow both to make a proper contribution (see section after next).

Mechanically Altering Probability

Suppose we add put a marble inside ball 33 of the "Ping-Pong balls" used to select lottery numbers. This would make ball 33 heavier than the others and much less likely to reach the top and be captured. The number 33 would not occur in the winning lottery numbers (not nearly as often, at least). Suppose the marble weighed eight grams. Can we simply factor this weight into the probability formula

$$P33 = 1/45 - 8 \qquad\qquad ???$$

This is really comparing apples to kumquats. Although the formula would give a lower score for the probability of number 33 occurring in the winning lottery numbers, it would not give the correct score. The weight in grams is directly related to the probability the ball will remain air borne and thus its chances of being selected, but the relationship is not nearly so simple.   A probability could not be calculated from the weight without some empirical studies.

If we knew, for example, that four grams lowered the probability from 1/45 or P = .0222 to, say, 1/3,600 or P = .0002778, we could guess four grams lowered the probability by a factor of about 100 (actually, 79.91). Would eight grams lower it (from the original .0222) by a factor of 200 or 1000? Probably neither, since the relationship also includes air currents and so forth and is probably not linear.

Calculated Values for Addiction Factors

If we cannot even calculate the effect of a marble in a bowl of Ping-Pong balls, how can I claim to have done such calculations with the complicated phenomenon of drug addiction? The answer is that I didn't! I did not calculate components of the equation for the probability of addiction (the components of P_s and P_i, according to Chapters 1 and 2) from physical factors. I observed that, as a rule, some factors seemed more likely to cause drug addiction than other factors and some chemical substances seemed more addicting than others.

I assigned values to the components, keeping two requirements in mind. First, the value for a component had to correctly rank it among similar components. Morphine, for example, had to have a higher value than iced tea for causing drug addiction. Second, the values had to make a proper contribution to the whole. A bad environment, for example, may be "very likely" to help someone become a drug addict, but it does not ensure it, since others in the same environment do not become addicted. Remembering that probability can never be greater than one, assigning a value of .80 to the environment would therefore not be reasonable.

The numbers assigned to various components in this book are not sacred. While I believe that, taken together, they give a very good estimate of the probability of addiction, I simply do not have the tools to precisely measure each component and eliminate all influence from others. That kind of resolution may have to wait for the arrival of the Starship Enterprise.

What is important for this theory of drug addiction is that certain additive components do exist and summing these components can give a total probability of addiction.

Predictive Value of Probability Theory

Assume for a moment that each component of both "equations"

$$P_s := P_c + P_r + P_p \qquad \text{(Chapter 1)}$$
$$P_i := P_g + P_m + P_e \qquad \text{(Chapter 2)}$$

have been determined to the tenth decimal place. Using the basic formula

$$P_a := P_s + P_i \qquad \text{(Introduction)},$$

we arrive at a score $P_a = 1.0$ that Mary, injecting half a grain of morphine intravenously, will become addicted. Will Mary become a drug addict?

This leads us to another common misconception about probability. Let us again start with the less-complicated lottery. Suppose we buy three lottery tickets, each of which has a chance of winning of 1/3. The probability of winning on any *one* ticket (out of the three) is 1/3 + 1/3 + 1/3, which equals 1. Since an event with a probability of 1 must always occur, we win, right?

Sorry. Although the mathematics implies this, it may not happen.[19] Statisticians like to say probability works only with a large sample and is guaranteed only when the sample reaches infinity. To have even a 50:50 chance of winning a $2 million lottery, plan on buying $50 million worth of $1 tickets! If you buy 1,000 of these dollar tickets, you could get close to the predicted number of wins: 333, or 1/3 of 1,000 (mostly $1 prizes). Even this, however, is not guaranteed: for a mathematically small (but personally expensive) sample of 1,000 tickets, you would probably win somewhere between 300 and 370 times.

---

[19] Of course, if we bought every possible combination of numbers we would have to win. Randomly buying the same number of tickets, however, does not guarantee it.

The point of this book is that we can say that Pat, who has a value for P_i of .50, is a good candidate for drug addiction if se is ever exposed to certain chemicals (see Table 2). There is a good chance of addiction, but it is not certain.

Appendix B
Chemistry

This appendix gives a quick course in the naming of drugs, the chemistry of solutions, organic structure, drug action, and how we might design drugs for a specific purpose. What it does not do is tell exactly how to manufacture controlled substances: I want to explain, not increase, the probability of addiction!

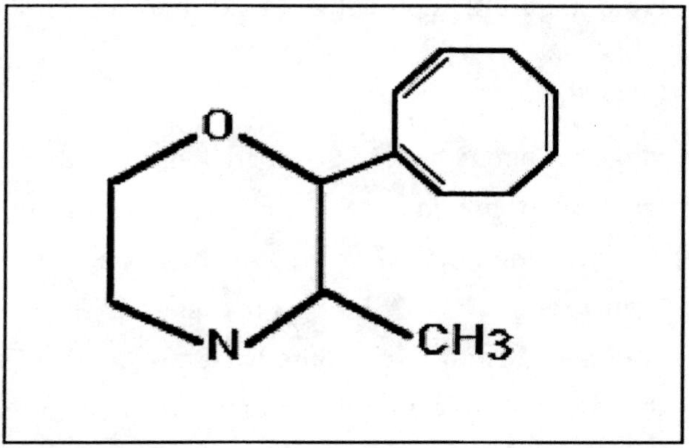

Figure 2.   Phenmetrazine Molecule

Drug Nomenclature

This appendix does not give the rigorous rules for naming organic compounds for two reasons. First, there are good, short explanations of organic nomenclature in references such as the CRC Handbook (CRCH92). Second, the terms usually used for a drug do not meet the requirements of the International Union of Pure and Applied Chemistry (IUPAC); they are not really proper scientific names.

The plethora of names for one substance can be confusing. Even the so-called scientific name for a drug typically uses some base form and tacks on other things to represent side chains (an organic term for any structure not in the main or parent chain) or simply some distinguishing term. Figure 2 shows the chemical structure of a stimulant popular among speed freaks.

(The strange hexagons are six-membered rings with a carbon atom at each vertex. If there are alternating lines inside the ring, it is "aromatic," a benzene ring. The ring in the upper, right corner of Figure 2, is an example. Although this special structure is drawn with alternating single and double bonds, all six bonds of the hexagon are "hybridized" to equivalent structures. Unless something else is shown attached to a vertex, a hydrogen atom is connected to each carbon.)

The drug represented in Figure 2 is called Preludin by the manufacturer and trademark holder Boehringer Ingelheim (and by many addicts). The "generic" drug name is phenmetrazine hydrochloride.

The more descriptive chemical name is 3-methyl-2-phenylmorpholine. The exact chemical name is 3-methyl-2-phenyl-2,3,5,6-tetrahydro-1,4-oxazine. This gives a hierarchy, from trademark to chemical, of ever longer names (box 12, for example).

Preludin™

phenmetrazine (hydrochloride)

3-methyl-2-phenyl-morpholine (hydrochloride)

3-methyl-2-phenyl-2,3,5,6-tetrahydro-1,4-oxazine (hydrochloride)

---

12. Typical Hierarchy of Drug Names

The last line should make it clear why drugs are assigned simple names and why even their "chemical" name is not very explicit. Physicians and pharmacists would have no time for insurance forms if they had to keep up with complete chemical names for thousands of substances. Phenmetrazine is a relatively simple drug. The rigorous chemical name of some steroids, antibiotics, and even common vitamins would each require a separate appendix!

Note that the "hydrochloride" is given in parentheses in the chemical names. The implication is not strictly correct, since a drug either is a hydrochloride or it is not. This is, however, consistent with the listing of the basic form of the drug in references such as the Merck Index (MERC89). To locate this drug, we look up the basic form; the explanation will also cover the hydrochloride form. This "hydrochloride" concept is important to drug addicts; the next section explains why.

Solution Chemistry for Drugs

A television report identified crack as "a highly addictive form of cocaine." Although "crack" is a different form of cocaine, we want to be clear that it is still cocaine. Crack is the most addictive form by only a slight margin, if at all.

Cocaine's simplest chemical name is benzoylmethylecgonine, described as a compound that forms slightly greasy monoclinic "crystals" that sublimates (turns to a gas without becoming liquid) at 98° Centigrade. In the hydrochloride form, it is soluble in water, forming a solution with pH = 4.5. Figure 3 shows the chemical structure of the base.

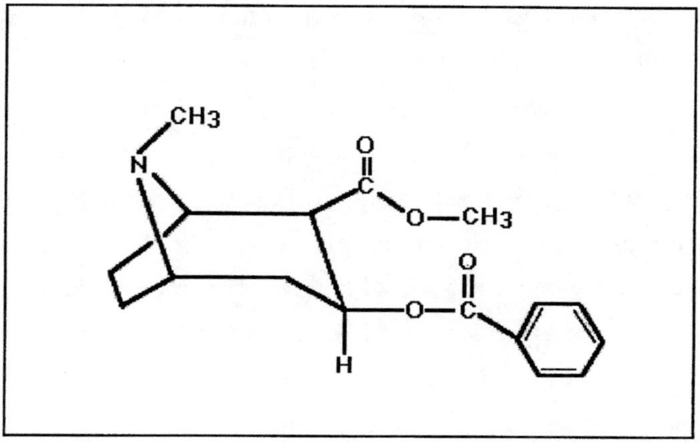

Figure 3.   Cocaine Molecule (as base)

When mixed in stoichiometric (a technical way of saying "the right") proportions with hydrochloric acid (HCl), benzoylmethylecgonine adds a hydrogen (H) ion to the nitrogen (N), giving the molecule shown above a positive charge. This is counteracted by the negative charge on the chlorine (Cl) ion. In this form, cocaine is much more stable, forms cleaner (non-greasy) crystals, can be crushed into a fine powder, and dissolves much more readily in water. This is the cocaine hydrochloride needle-using addicts like to inject.

Sulfuric acid makes the base form water soluble by a similar mechanism, forming sulfates. In the drug world, amphetamine sulfate is not common.

The opposite of an acid is a base or alkali. Just as we could make the hydrochloride of cocaine by mixing the base form with hydrochloric acid, we can change the hydrochloride form back to the base form by mixing the hydrochloride form with a base. Addicts commonly use baking soda, chemically sodium bicarbonate, which is a mildly basic and also not too dangerous if excess baking soda is used.

We have to get highly technical for just one paragraph. There are several definitions of *acid* and *base* (or alkali) in chemistry. A common definition is a measure called pH, which is the logarithm of the reciprocal of the concentration of H ions. This means pH goes *down* by 1 for each 10-time increase in H+ ions. Acids have a pH less than 7.0, bases have a pH greater than 7.0, and pure water has a pH exactly 7.0. The base form of cocaine has a pH slightly greater than 7, and the hydrochloride form has a pH of 4.5.

The *base* form of the drug may not always be basic in the sense that it has a pH greater than 7. Perhaps it is best to consider the base form more as a platform for constructing other forms of the drug. Although pH provides an absolute scale, acidity and alkalinity can be relative to each other. Relative to hydrochloric and sulfuric acid, almost everything is "basic."

Freshman chemistry instructors tell classes to remember the rule "Like dissolves like," meaning that ionic compounds like sodium chloride (table salt) dissolve in polar compounds like water. Organic compounds like bubble gum dissolve in organic solvents like acetone, benzene, and gasoline (mostly heptane). Drugs are organic compounds, many of which can be made ionic by the addition of an acid such as hydrochloric or sulfuric. (The drug must have a free electron pair, such as a nitrogen or carbonyl: most drugs have such a structure. Adding the acid to a pure hydrocarbon like gasoline will not work, and will occasionally explode!)

The base form of the cocaine dissolves very well in "organic" solvents such as ether. The gooey base solution is dried, and perhaps mixed it with a crystalline substance such as sucrose, until it is hard. Any quantity much over a gram cracks open during processing, perhaps the source of the street moniker "crack."

Freebasing, another use for the base form of cocaine, has been mostly replaced by smoking crack. Free-basing involved dissolving the base cocaine in ether, putting the solution on a nicotine or marijuana cigarette, allowing the ether to evaporate, and smoking the result. Freebasing is extremely dangerous! Due to the inflammability of ethyl ether (and perhaps the inpatience of addicts), the ether may not have completely evaporated from the cigarette. Igniting any quantity of ether fumes is a trip no one needs.

Sources of Drugs

Where do we get drugs? (No, this is not a list of dealers.) Since people were using mood-altering substances well before there were bioengineering firms, some drugs obviously must occur naturally. This is also a natural conclusion in light of Axiom 1 and the fact that we evolved in this world. Caffeine, the drug of tea and coffee, is one of a class of plant alkaloids, a category that also includes cocaine, morphine, codeine, and numerous drugs such as quinine that are not abused.

The physiological effects of caffeine, one of the weaker of the alkaloids, include vasodilatation, pupillary dilation, increased heart rate. It is a stimulant, increasing the rate (and some say quality) of mental functioning. These effects are significant: one cup of strong coffee given to a child who has never had any can produce symptoms mimicking hyperactivity, even though most children have a tolerance due to extensive caffeine exposure in the form of chocolate. Withdrawal from amounts of caffeine as little as 200 mg./day causes tiredness and a feeling of puffy eyes for about a week. Withdrawal from heavy use (1200 mg/day) can cause headaches, leg cramps, extreme tiredness, and even depression lasting several months.

In spite of what addicts would like to believe, caffeine is mood altering and addicting. As with tobacco, misinformation abounds. After all, there is good money to be made selling addictive products. (See GILB76 for more information on caffeine addiction.)

The opium poppy contains several addicting substances. Besides various sticky tars and impurities, the gooey exudate from the opium poppy contains several addicting substances (Box 13).

morphine	10 - 16 %
noscapine	4 - 8 %
codeine	0.8 - 2.5 %
papaverine	0.5 - 2.5 %
thebaine	.5 - 2 %

Raw (i.e., unprocessed) opium also contains about 15 more alkaloids, meconic acid, some lactic and sulfuric acids, sugar, resinous and wax-like substances, and water (MERC89).

13. Composition of Opium

Pharmacology

Axiom 1 states that all addicting drugs replace a substance produced naturally within the body. We assume this replacement mechanism, direct or indirect, lies at the bottom of all addictive substance pharmacology. Since it is primary to understanding addiction, the mechanism of this replacement is explained in Chapter 1 rather than in an appendix. This section delves into replacement from the drug side: what drug structures are likely to produce addicting substances? This section also covers relative strengths of drugs, which gives rise to the hierarchy presented in the tables of Chapter 1.

First, we need to define "drug activity." Does zidovudine (AZT) help an AIDS patient? "Help" is not an exact term: there must be some empirical means of measuring what the drug accomplishes. Double blind studies (defined in Appendix D) are generally needed to prove the utility of a drug because patients who want to be helped will sometimes get better with sugar tablets. To prove it "works," the company must demonstrate to the satisfaction of the Food and Drug Administration that AZT prolongs the life of an AIDS patient. Quality of life is certainly a valid criterion, but it must be quantified in some way such as "reduction of nausea from daily to once a week."

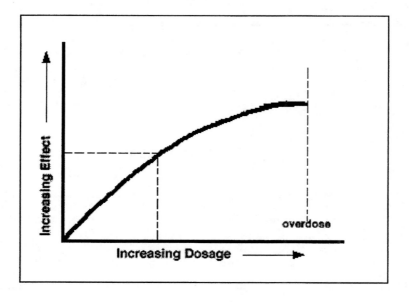

Figure 4. Dose-Response Curve

Let us assume we have an exact method for measuring a drug effect like *sedation*: perhaps the failure of subject to respond to electric shock. We measure this for two drugs, getting numbers 35 and 40 volts, for example. Suppose we give the two drugs together. Does this reduce the response, which now requires 75 volts to elicit?

Drugs can act concurrently in four different ways: independent, additive, subtractive, or synergistic. In the independent "interaction," the drug effects are unrelated: taking erythromycin and aspirin together for a sinus infection is an example. In reality, few drug interactions are completely independent in all effects: acetylsalicylic acid (aspirin) and erythromycin both upset the stomach. This undesirable side effect could preclude their use together before the therapy is completed.

Drug effects can be additive or subtractive when the drugs do almost exactly the same thing or have exactly the opposite effect. If I took 50 milligrams of sodium phenobarbital and 50 milligrams of sodium pentobarbital, which differ only in the length of their sedative effect, I would be approximately twice as sleepy as I would be with 50 milligrams of either drug alone. If I took 50 milligrams of phenobarbital and 5 milligrams of methamphetamine, I would feel virtually nothing. Methamphetamine is a perfect antagonist for barbiturates: the effects are opposite and methamphetamine can serve as an antedote for an overdose of any barbiturate.

The dangerous drug interaction is the synergistic mechanism, where the whole is more than the sum of the parts. Ethyl alcohol and barbiturates are the perfect example of this effect. If the two ounces of (pure) alcohol produce sedation of 40 on our scale and 150 milligrams of sodium phenobarbital rates 60, the two ounces of alcohol and 150 milligrams of phenobarbital might give a number of 140. If I increase the amount of both the alcohol and barbiturate to less than half the lethal doses for each, the shock necessary to wake me could well go to infinity. I could die.

Since addicts may seek a particular drug effect, they might well take drugs with similar effects whose interactions are additive or synergistic. The results are often tragic. One addict read the caution on his Darvon bottle: Warning may cause drowsiness. Alcohol may intensify this effect. Assuming the alcohol might intensify all the effects, he drank a six-pack of beer with it. Attempting to drive home, he started onto the freeway via a typical entrance ramp, but did not recognize where to drive: he crossed both lanes, the median, and both lanes of the oncoming traffic.

Pharmacology also deals with a somewhat non-intuitive concept. People "know" that taking more pills increases the effect: if one is good, two are better. This is not strictly true. Two aspirin (acetylsalicylic acid) have almost twice the pain relieving ability of one aspirin. Four aspirin, however, do *not* have twice the pain relieving ability of two aspirin, even though the larger amount may make the effect last longer. The ability of a drug to cause a particular effect approaches a limit beyond which further amounts are not only ineffective but dangerous. You could take enough aspirin to kill you without reaching the pain-killing power of 62.5 mg. (a *grain*) of morphine. The ability of a drug to cause a particular effect is called its *efficacy*.

We have compared aspirin and morphine, finding the morphine more efficacious in relieving pain. Suppose, however, we compare tabun, a nerve "gas" (actually, a red liquid when cold or under pressure) and ethyl alcohol (the common intoxicant in beer and whiskey).

Tabun can kill in several parts per million in about seven seconds. Assuming sufficient air movement, half an ounce of tabun would kill all 60,000 people in a domed sports stadium in less than a minute. One person can drink half an ounce of ethyl alcohol and barely notice the effects. At one sporting event, however, our 60,000-person crowd might use 200,000 ounces of ethyl alcohol (meaning many should take the bus home).

The differences in the amount of drugs required to cause the effect– whatever that effect is – is called *potency*.

Both efficacy and potency are relevant to addiction and very important to addicts. The efficacy of a drug for altering mood (in some manner the addict likes) determines the order of Table 2 (Chapter 2). Potency is relevant because a junkie would not like to shoot two pints of liquid to get high. Speed freaks "cook down" (evaporate the liquid) their hit to increase the "rush" (the immediate pleasurable effect from the injection). Potency presents an ever-present danger to many addicts because of its unpredictability for street drugs.

Although efficacy cannot be changed without changing the chemical substance, potency can be effectively altered by route of administration. In my example above, I assumed the subject drank the half-ounce of alcohol; injecting it would result in extreme intoxication very quickly. (Intravenous injection of one-half ounce of ethyl alcohol would probably not kill, but it would bring a person dangerously close to the often-lethal concentration of .5 percent blood alcohol.)[20]

---

20 The numbers in the last few paragraphs are reasonably accurate. There is, however, a wide range of responses even in normal individuals to drug dosages. Addiction, with its tolerance and occasional paradoxical reaction, introduces even more variance.

Designing Drugs

As with other sections in the appendix, this section seeks to describe in a few pages a subject to which entire libraries are devoted. Many of these libraries are proprietary–owned exclusively by a drug firm–and are probably more carefully guarded than most FBI files. Nevertheless, this discussion sufficient for understanding the principle of designing drugs.

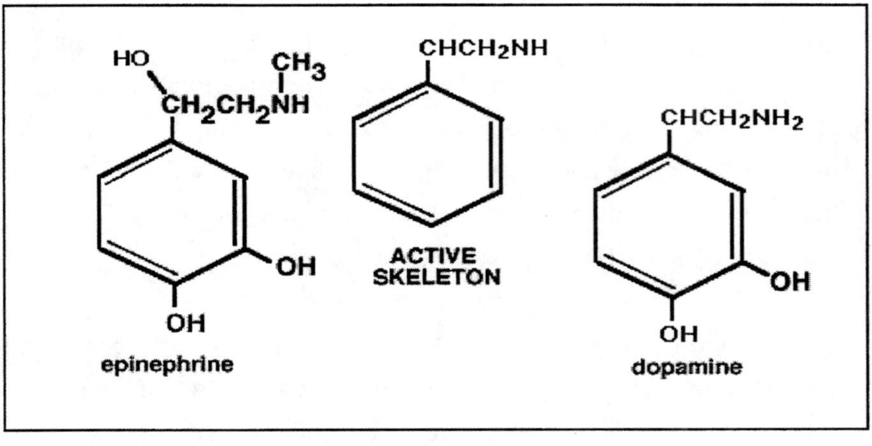

Figure 5.   Epinephrine/Dopamine Skeleton

Underground chemists, some of whom are quite adept, use these same principles to make the "designer drugs" sold on the streets. The purpose in their case is often not to improve the potency or efficacy of the drug, but to design a substance with the same effects of another addicting drug that is sufficiently different in chemical structure so that it is not illegal (unaware that the Controlled Substances Act allows for quick addition of other drugs to the categories).

Even if the main purpose is not be to increase the potency of the drug, the chemist may do so accidentally. Whether the increased potency is intended or "serendipitous," the effect on the unwary addict is the same: half a teaspoon of street heroin may barely slow downl a seasoned addict; half a teaspoon of α-methyl fentanyl could kill several horses.

How would we design a drug? First, we must have something to aim at. Although the drug companies probably have computer design tools I am not even aware of, the designer usually cannot take the structure of an active site in the body and "fit" a drug structure to that site. (In fact, most active sites are discovered after we know a drug affects them.)

Our model is a substance, already thoroughly investigated, having at least some of the properties we want. Beginning with this model, the chemist adds and removes substituents – chains of atoms that act chemically as a single unit– from the "parent" molecule (the original substance). Let's consider a class of stimulant drugs, using a neuro-transmitter skeleton as a model. Figure 5 shows neurotransmitters dopamine and epinepherine and a skeleton they share: a two-carbon chain with a benzene ring at one end and an amine group at the other. Dopamine is a brain transmitter; I will concentrate on the more ubiquitous epinepherine.

Epinephrine is produced naturally in the huwan body by the small adrenal glands atop the kidneys. When we detect an emergency, the sympathetic nervous system stimulates the adrenal glands to release epinephrine into the bloodstream. Immediately, heart rate shoots up and blood flow is cut drastically to the skin surface and to body systems such as the digestive tract that can be put on hold. The brain and muscles are at DEFCON 4 – ready for nuclear war. This is the "fight or flight" reaction.

Even though a number of addicts have obtained and injected epinephrine, it never became an abused drug. The unfortunate addicts reported falling to the floor, back arched as in the classic picture of a seizure or ECT, turning white all over (the loss of blood to the skin), and foaming at the mouth. They remembered little more of their "high" than an epileptic might remember of a seizure.

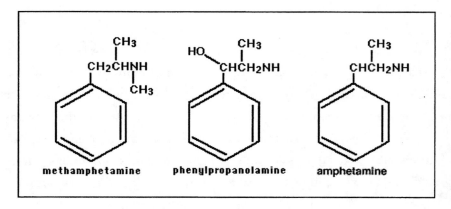

Figure 6. Three Representative Stimulants

Compare the scary scenario just described to the effects of methamphetamine, whose chemical structure is shown in Figure 6. "Meth" is one of the most addicting compounds ever discovered or prepared. In a vulnerable individual, one "good" hit (injection) may cause addiction for life. (If se has a good supply of methamphetamine, "life" is about two years.) As can be seen from Figures 5 and 6, meth is closely related to epinephrine.

What is the critical difference? There really is no easy answer to this. The situation is similar to filing some metal from a key so it fits a little better into a lock (refer to Figure 1). The active skeleton in Figure 5 is common to epinephrine, methamphetamine, and a large number of related stimulants, including phenmetrazine (in Figure 2, it is part of the ring containing the oxygen and nitrogen).

As we see with the differences between epinephrine and methamphetamine, removing and adding substituents changes the physiological effect. This change is not major in the examples given in Figure 5, since all structures are those of stimulant drugs, but it is important. An addict who injected phenylpropanolamine (as pure hydrochloride) reported little psychic effects such as those of methamphetamine, but felt he had been "kicked in the chest by a mule." This compound raises blood pressure; injecting it did so quite rapidly. The addict was restless and unable to sleep, but not "high": he had gotten all bad effects of "speed" with none of the good effects he sought.

This is the basic the idea of how drugs are designed. This model (or any other for that matter) does not show the whole picture, however. The synthetic narcotic Demerol™ acts like codeine and heroin, yet its chemical structure does not even slightly resemble either. A cursory search would reveal several very dangerous chemicals with the skeleton for epinephrine shown in Figure 5. A lot more data are no doubt available in the proprietary literature of drug companies, but many facets of the physiological activity of drugs are simply not known yet.

Appendix C
Genetics

As typically taught, genetics deals with the physical and chemical structure of chromosomes, genes, deoxyribonucleic acid (DNA), ribonucleic acid (RNA), and how all these are related. When the genetics course does come to the topic of inheritance, it deals with F1 and F2 generations, homozygotes, heterozygotes, and (if the student is particularly unlucky) chromosome mapping. There is precious little in a genetics course about exactly what is inherited.

Genetics cannot be fairly treated without a brief explanation of some biochemical mechanisms. Although our concentration should be on inheritance, exactly what is inherited is known in only a few relatively straightforward cases. This appendix shows how a predisposition toward addiction might be inherited. Please remain aware that it is far from proven that addiction is hereditary. This appendix also discusses how a trait can"run in the family" and still not necessarily be hereditary.

Genes and Chromosomes

Most huwan beings have 23 pairs of chromosomes. Except for sperm and egg cells, each cell of the body has exactly the same 23 pairs. The sperm and egg cells have 23 chromosomes, but they are not paired. When they join at conception, the potential person has 23 chromosomes from the mother and 23 from the father. This system does not always work perfectly and several genetic diseases result from malfunctions. (Most malfunctions in genetic material are fatal before even a minimum fetus can develop.)

Each chromosome is a strand of deoxyribonucleic acid (DNA), which is a series of base pairs. There are four DNA bases: adenine (A), guanine (G), cytosine (C), and thiamine (T). Adenine always pairs with thiamine and guanine with cytosine. A portion of DNA is often represented as follows

```
A- T- T- T- C- G- C- T–T–T- C- G- C
 |  |  |  |  |  |  |  |  |  |  |  |  |
T- A- A- A- G- C- G- A- A- A- G- C- G
```

Each base is connected to a polypeptide, a sugar molecule with a phosphorus atom attached. With the polypeptides on the outside and the base pairs on the inside, the DNA is three-dimensionally the famous double helix.

Each DNA strand has thousands of genes, each composed of a dozen to several hundred DNA base pairs. The gene is considered the unit of heredity and takes different forms, each of which is responsible for a different characteristic. These forms are called alleles. There is, for instance, an allele for blue eyes and an allele for brown eyes. Either allele is considered the same gene. Since chromosomes occur in pairs, there are two alleles for the same trait. They can be the same or different. Using the eye color gene, and three combinations are possible:

> blue-blue
> blue-brown
> brown-brown.

Although these are all possible combinations, it is somewhat misleading. One allele comes from the father and one from the mother (except for some sex-linked characteristics occurring on the X chromosome-we will skip these), mixed in a totally random fashion. This means there are actually two ways the alleles can be different:

> 1. blue (from father)   – brown (from mother)
> 2. brown (from father)   – blue (from mother).

Although the effect is the same whichever parent supplies the particular allele, the proportions are different. The fact that the blue-brown pair can arise two ways means 50 percent of the offspring will have this pair, 25 percent blue-blue, and 25 percent brown-brown.

One notation in genetics can be a source of confusion. Traits determined by an allele are typically designated by the first letter of the dominant trait, whatever letter the recessive trait begins with. Since "brown" and "blue" because both begin with "b," so, red hair, which is recessive in people to both brown and black hair color. Comparing black and red hair alleles, we "B" for black hair and "b," not "R" or "r," for red hair. (Ignore hair colors like blond, brown, and punk orange in this analysis.)

If two people had mixed alleles for black-red hair color, both would have a genotype of Bb. Using this notation to examine the possibilities for a child of these two people, we have the following four allele combinations (genotype), with the actual hair color (phenotype) in the right column:

BB black hair
Bb black hair
bB black hair
bb red hair

This is the famous 75 percent ratio for the F2 generation. F2 is the offspring of two parents with opposite, pure alleles for some trait. One parent of the F1 generation was BB and produced only B gametes and the other parent was bb, producing only b gametes. Their offspring, the F2 generation, must be mixed allele: Bb. Three quarters of the offspring will have the dominant trait, black hair in this case, and one quarter will have the recessive trait of red hair.

Understanding the Genetic Code

Strictly speaking, it is not a gene that "causes" alcoholism or anything else, but one form of a particular gene. Except unusual conditions such as trisomy 21 (Down's syndrome), everyone has the same genes. The different forms of a gene are known as alleles. It is the mixture of alleles that causes blue eyes, brown hair, or the tendency toward addiction. Except for the sex chromosomes, people have two of every gene, one from each parent.

Both genes can have the same allele (homozygous) or different alleles (heterozygous), giving three possibilities for a relatively-simple trait such as blue eyes. If both alleles are blue, the person will have blue eyes. If both are brown, the person will have brown eyes. We must now introduce the concept of dominance. For eye color, brown is completely dominant and blue (completely) recessive. If one allele says "blue" and the other says "brown," the person will have brown eyes. (The collie with one blue and one brown eye is not the usual result of mixing alleles!)

Eye color is an expressed characteristic of genetic makeup. Seldom is such a clear expression available. If two genes are needed to determine the trait, each with two possible alleles, there are 16 possibilities for allele combinations. Although this 16-condition grid appears in most biology texts, most traits are not even this simple. An allele can be partially dominant, co-dominant, or not dominant at all (with the reverse true in each case for recessive).

To sort out this additional complication, we must see how the gene makes its presence felt: how the genetic information is expressed.

Gene Expression

An allele of a gene is one of several possible blueprints. The building constructed from the allele blueprint is a protein. A collection of the same proteins is tissue. A mass of identical (or functionally related) tissue is an organ. A combination of the proper organs is a living organism. Of course, the DNA does contain the "code" for the organism, but the relationship is neither simple nor straightforward.

As explained earlier, we have two alleles for every trait. (Exceptions are in some chromosomal aberrations and sex-linked characteristics.) If one allele makes a vital protein, the other could be defective and the organism might still survive.

An interesting case of this is sickle-cell anemia. This disease, occurring predominately in Negroes, is marked by warped red blood cells, which take on a sickle shape. The malformed cells block capillaries, causing poor circulation, great pain, and often death. The sickle-cell trait is carried by a recessive allele.

If many people with sickle-cell anemia die, why was the disease not naturally eliminated from the population long ago? As explained in the first section of this appendix, both alleles must be recessive for the recessive trait to be expressed. When one allele is sickle-cell and the other normal, the person has some malformed blood cells and many sickle-shaped cells. Such a person is resistant to malaria. The "disease" of sickle-cell anemia, not fully expressed, is beneficial in certain climates (such as Africa).

It is possible such a situation occurs with addiction. Suppose we postulate a gene for compulsion. Those having one type of allele (both the same) are obcessed about everything, often to the point of psychosis. Such a person has a high P_i, and can become a drug addict if exposed to the right substance.

How about a person with one compulsion allele? Such an individual might be an excellent student, a hard worker, a devoted spouse. Se might be persistent about achieving goals, but not a "do it at any cost" type. This genetic structure is likely beneficial and the gene will remain in the population.[21]

Let me repeat over again and then another time that a complicated behavior like drug addiction is probably not controlled by a single gene. Partial expression of a single, recessive allele fits the addiction profile more closely, but this is still likely to be a simplification. Using multiple alleles, all partially expressed and interactive, we might have a viable genetic model.

---

[21] Modern wan has not been around long enough to do any evolving. It takes thousands of years to make any changes. Natural selection is not likely to affect people anyway, since we feel the need to encourage every person, however genetically flawed, to reproduce.

Pedigree Studies

Figure 7 is an example of a pedigree chart, showing a trait such as pattern baldness that shows up principally in males. (Pattern baldness does happen in females: if we prepared the chart for enough generations, we would see an example.) The chart is constructed using information about individuals in all families involved in the history of an individual such as 3-1 (first offspring in third generation). Every aunt, uncle and grandparent is checked for the trait. Although the process can tolerate some gaps, there are genetic patterns that show up only in pedigree charts that completely cover more than three generations.

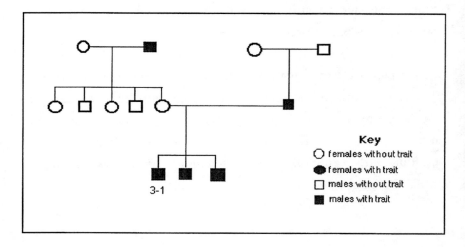

Key
○ females without trait
● females with trait
□ males without trait
■ males with trait

Figure 7. Typical Chart for an Inherited Trait

In formal genetics, a pedigree study is an attempt to discover the pattern of some trait in the subject's ancestors. It is not related in any way to "purity" of the race or eugenics. Geneticists stole a form of family tree from the anthropologists, representing females by a circle and males by a square. Those individuals expressing the trait have their symbol colored in; those without the trait must be content with an outline. If a chart can be accurately constructed for three or more generations, all sorts of things can be discovered from examining it.

Such a pedigree chart can be very useful for analysis of a trait: students in graduate genetics courses are given such charts on tests and asked to determine complicated patterns of inheritance such as a trait whose gene is on the X chromosome. (The X, or male, chromosome is small and contains few genes. Most sex-linked traits come from the female parent.)

We can use a carefully researched pedigree chart to decide if some characteristic is hereditary. If we marked individuals who owned blue cars, for example, we would see an erratic pattern fitting no known rules of genetics (unless, of course, the tendency to buy a blue car is hereditary). For pattern baldness or blue eyes, the charts show a clear hereditary influence.

But suppose we make a chart for a behavior such as violent criminality, tendency to physically abuse others, or drug addiction? In many cases, pedigree charts do show inheritance of the behavior. But are these behaviors genetic? Is the criminal a criminal because se inherited some tendency from har parents, or because se was continually neglected and beaten by parents who in turn were similarly treated by their parents?

The inheritance of blue eyes is easy: it is due to a single gene and it is obvious whether the person has the quality. Down's syndrome, for example, is caused by a single, extra chromosome (trisomy 21). Even this genetically simple mechanism was not understood until the middle of the Twentieth century. When we deal with huwan genetics, we must wait until some trait shows up and then examine the data. Doing breeding experiments on huwans, as Hitler discovered, is politically unpopular.

The Politics of Genetics

The Huwan Genome Project is one of the most intense endeavors ever taken up by wankind. Its object is to map every gene in all huwan chromosomes. In the United States, discussions have begun about the social effects of such knowledge. Would insurance companies, for example, using genetic information to reject certain individuals as high risk? No doubt they would try. And what if it turns out, God of the liberals forbid, that races really do differ in intelligence, aggressiveness, or tendency toward drug addiction?

In 1869, Francis Galton published <u>Hereditary Genius</u> in which he said that great intelligence runs in families. He advocated eugenic programs in which society would control reproduction to gradually improve the huwan race. After the Nazi attempt to "improve the huwan race," most people do not even want to hear the word eugenics. What part does heredity play in huwan behavior?

In 1969, Arthur Jensen claimed that intelligence was about 80 percent hereditary. It was known that some races scored lower on classic IQ tests than other races. Putting these two together produced the conclusion that one race may not be as intelligent as another. (In the 1990's, it is considered politically incorrect to even discuss this question, leaving the possible problem without a chance of solution.)

Jensen's work caused controversy at the level of Darwin's publication of The Origin of Species. Some genuine scientists and many liberals who simply did not like the data questioned Jensen's reasoning (KAGA69, LEWO76, MACK84). While genetics might account for differences within one race, the differences between race were more likely due to environment (EYSE81). Some claimed the IQ tests were culturally biased (MERC71), although later work showed this was probably a weak effect (KAPL85, OAKL85). A similar political disturbance occurred when sociobiology hinted that behavior such as altruism or antisocial behavior might also be genetic (WILS77).

So we now have politically correct science. When liberals feel they must justify a behavior such as homosexuality, they embrace any study suggesting a hereditary factor. When the tests indicate one race might be less intelligent than another, liberals reject the evidence. No examination of the data is allowed; it is rejected simply because the concept does not fit someone's image of how the world should be. Olympics have been going on for over 2000 years, yet the male-dominated culture allowed women to run in marathons only very recently. Evidence had already shown that females probably have more endurance than males.

More recently, John Horgan examined the inheritance of behaviors such as intelligence, homosexuality, and addiction (HORG93). A genetic basis for such complicated behavior, Mr. Horgan contends, is simply not conclusive. I do not believe Mr. Horgan completely proves his point, since IQ is generally considered at least 50 percent hereditary–due to genetic influence. I do, however, feel that the politicization of genetics can have terrible consequences (reference: anything from Nazi Germany).

I do not wish to take sides in a violent politically-correct controversy. I want "only" to defend the scientific method and the right to examine data unhindered by politics. Scientific principles of observation and testing have (for the most part) dispelled the idea that the earth is flat. As we near the end of the 20th Century, however, there still are people who demand that "Creationism" (a completely mythical fantasy) be taught alongside evolution. And there are educated people, in positions of power and responsibility, that will not look at data because they do not like what the data show.

Shortly after the year 2000, all 46 huwan chromosomes will be mapped. Although the function of many genes may still elude us, we will be in a better position to objectively consider the inheritance of complicated genetic traits. At that time, we will be in a better position to evaluate the old adage that drug addiction "runs in families" (and whether or not that effect is due more to genes than environment). At present, it *seems* that a tendency toward drug addiction is inherited.

Appendix D
Psychology

This appendix explains some terminology of psychology as it relates to the ideas in this book. The first three sections cover concepts relevant to addiction. The final section is a glossary defining the terms. Definitions are necessarily short: as with many ideas presented here, there are whole libraries about the subject. Consistent with the text of the book, which concerns itself with observation, measurement, and prediction, as opposed to basic theory, I deal only tangentially with underlying mechanisms.

I am not assailing such theory. I simply do not know why some choose the use of an addicting drug over other coping behaviors. Learning psychologists and psychotherapists can perhaps help with the reasons. Such theory is more the province of pure psychology than of my "technological" predictive presentation.

Learning Theory

Opposing the old Freudian school, a group of psychologists known as behaviorists decided that studying what went on in our heads was lots of fun, but not particularly relevant to learning. The foremost proponent of this idea, B. F. Skinner, believed the sole determining factor of behavior is the reinforcement we receive for performing the act. Reinforcement can be anything the organism perceives as positive: contrary to some popular beliefs, it does not have to be food. An affectionate pat on the head may work for your dog.

Since most animals spend a good part of their lives looking for food, however, food is a good reinforcer. The frequency with which we feed the dog is very important for learning. If we want our dog to do something, we try to finagle har into doing it and then give har a dog biscuit "immediately" afterward. (*Immediately* is defined later.) If we give a dog biscuit every time the dog does this behavior, we are reinforcing the behavior 100 percent.

Suppose we only feed the dog every *other* time se performs the behavior. Suppose we feed har every third or fourth time. These are called variable reinforcement schedules. There are two quantities that can be used to decide when the reward (reinforcement) is given. We can use the number of times the behavior has occured, every fourth time, for example. Or we can use time, providing the reinforcement every hour or so (assuming it is a behavior that happens half a dozen or so times per hour).

Variable reinforcement teaches the dog that if se is persistent enough, se will be rewarded. A behavior reinforced in this way will persist for a fairly long time after reinforcement is stopped: the behavior is not easily extinguished. The most effective schedule of all is to reward the dog at varying intervals of time. This is called a variable-interval reinforcement schedule. Using such a schedule, Dr. Skinner succeeded in getting rats to work for food (rather than rest) until they actually died from the effort.

To be effective (as a simple stimulus-response mechanism), reinforcement must occur within 30 seconds of the activity. For reinforcement, *immediately* is within 30 seconds of the act. If we wait longer than that, we are likely to reinforce a different (and perhaps unwanted) behavior. Negative reinforcement works exactly the same way: punishing an animal after more than 30 seconds is at best a waste of energy and at worst, cruel.

Drug use is one the most powerful reinforcement system ever designed: the variable-interval reinforcement schedule. In early stages of addiction, the user is rewarded, immediately and highly effectively, for taking the substance. As the drug user/addict gains tolerance for the drug, the reinforcement occurs on a more erratic schedule, depending not only on the physical condition of the addict but also the quality of the drug. Eventually, the reward may seldom occur, but the addict will work very hard to get it. A behavior reinforced in such a manner is very difficult to stop ("cure").

Mental Dysfunction

The old expression "mad as a hatter" comes from last century when workers who made hats used mercury in the processing. The mercury poisoning killed some workers, but it left many more seriously damaged mentally. Is insanity (when it can even be clearly defined) the result of some biological damage that can be fixed with the right drug? Is insanity genetic? Or is the insane person "derranged" in a manner that responds to sufficient "talk" therapy?

Although some experts might argue this, the classical school of mental disease began with Sigmund Freud (1856-1939). Before Freud, the insane were typically locked up and tortured in various ways. With the idea of the unconscious, Freud not only impressed his fellow physicians (eventually), but also captured the popular imagination. Why people do irrational things seemed more explainable: it was their unconscious or "id." (Please remember that naming something is not explaining it, and certainly not curing it.)

---

hebephrenic
> odd, silly, disassociated behavior
> (Government, for example)

catatonic
- body rigid, psyche cut off from sensory input

obsessive-compulsive
- fanatic repetition of behavior

paranoid
- delusions of persecution
- may believe se is Jesus Christ, Napoleon, Joan of Arc

---

14. Four Possible Categories of Psychosis

The totally insane were classified schizophrenic, meaning split psyche, even though the true multiple personality such as Norman Bates (PSYC60) is not even a common variety of schizophrenia (and certainly not common in the population). Box 14 shows four typical categories. Basic psychology texts may list additional categories and may leave out some shown in Box 14. (I have heard that Karl Menninger, psychiatrist and student of Sigmund Freud himself, would sometimes dismiss interns for classifying a patient as "schizophrenic.") Often, *schizophrenic* is used as a synonym for *psychotic.*; certainly the term is overworked.

Usually, maniac-depressive (extreme mood swings) is not considered schizophrenic, since the depressed or maniac person retains some contact with reality. The implication that the maniac-depressive is not as "insane" does not follow. The depressed person might lead a life of misery and constant physical ailments, while the classical paranoid might merrily go through life as Napoleon or Jesus Christ. (Maniac-depression is now called *bipolar disorder*. I have used the older term because this is still history.)

Historically, the psychoses were the serious mental illnesses. There were also neuroses such as phobias that were "inconvenient," but not debilitating. Although the terms neurosis (pl. neuroses) and psychosis (pl. psychoses) are still used, they are now usually looked upon as the same disease, just in different degrees. In this model, the "normal" person would worry se left the iron plugged in while going on vacation, the neurotic would return to the house several times to check, and the psychotic would become so obsessed se would iron everything in the house and never make it to the vacation.

This continuum is important for drug addiction. By virtually any definition, someone who has been without food or sleep for five days due to heavy use of methamphetamine is insane. The drug, however, did not exactly *cause* a psychosis. It shifted someone who already had mental difficulties (drug user with high P_i: see Chapter 2) toward the psychotic end of the spectrum. The popular expression "pushed har over the edge" is not really good, since it implies a monster under the surface waiting to escape. The completely psychotic meth/ice user seen in the emergency room is the combination of a powerful drug, the mental disfunction from lack of sleep and erratic blood sugar, and underlying mental problems in the addict.

Memory Loss

Modern authorities recognize several components in memory. Typically, psychology texts use three components of memory: encoding, retention, and recall. Since drugs can affect encoding at several points, at least four components are more useful in the context of this work: short-term formation, long-term formation, storage, and recall. (Evidence supports this four-component model: short-term memory seems to involve the limbic system whereas long-term memory is more holographic.) We might add a fifth component, especially when dealing with drug use: Did the subject even hear the statement?

To remember something, the person must somehow sense what is to be remembered and "store" it in short-term memory, probably chemical in nature. We can store only about seven units in short-term memory, which is why we might break up larger numbers into memorable groups. Difficulties in concentration, reported by addicts, indicate problems with short-term memory, and if the information is not encoded in the first place, it will not be there to be remembered.

Either the strength of the event (stimulus) or its repetition might make it part of long-term memory, which involves a change in the neuron interconnections within the brain. (Penfield has found increased amounts of white matter–nerve axons and dendrites–in the brains of rats following complicated learning tasks over "couch potato" controls.) Unless the brain is later damaged, long-term storage is permanent. The event is recorded, even if we cannot remember it precisely on cue.

Or are they? Great debate occurs around the idea that we can remember anything we ever experienced. Under hypnosis, an 80-year old subject might remember what se had for breakfast when se was three years old. This proves the existence of one old memory (provided, of course, it can be verified), but it does not prove every experience is "in there somewhere." Storage of a memory assumes there is no damage to the nerve cells of the brain, their interconnections, and neurotransmitters.

If the memory is intact, can we recall it? In repression, a person has a very vivid memory of some painful event such as a sibling being burned to death in a fire, but cannot remember it without hypnosis or psychotherapy. To a lesser extent, we usually refuse to dwell on painful memories, although we could remember them if asked. The association of painful emotion with an event is a barrier to recalling that event.

All these are relevant to drug addiction. There is evidence that alcohol and marijuana damage the short-term memory mechanism. Hallucinogens and narcotics that effectively remove a person from real sensory input block observation of phenomena going on around har. The event is not recorded (encoded) in the first place and of course cannot be remembered. One who continuously uses drugs, hallucinogenic or otherwise, may have to look at each digit of a phone number to dial it, being unable to commit the number to short-term memory.

Even if the addict can remember a phone number long enough to dial it, se will probably not do well in graduate school. "Everything seems a jumbled-up mess," is a complaint that might indicate difficulties in forming long-term memory. Some memory forms, as the addict can remember events during addiction, but it may be "out of sync" with the actual order of the events and pieces are missing.

Difficulties in recall also occur due to the painful emotional memories involved in ongoing drug addiction. Some confusion seems to straighten itself out when the addict stops using drugs and receives proper therapy, indicating problems with recall rather than memory formation. The memory is still damaged, however: the addict may become confidently certain of events that either did not happen or can be shown to have happened at a different time.

A hopeful note is that brain damage due to drugs is probably not the main reason for confusion and loss of memory. The Princeton student who entered law school with approximately half his brain removed because of a massive tumor testifies to the resilient, holographic nature of memory. A person can recover from even advanced stages of addiction and still function normally.

Selected Psychological Terms

The terms in this section are commonly used in psychology and are not specific to drug addiction. The definitions, of course, are oriented toward the term's use as it relates to drug addiction.

Anhedonia

Meaning literally "no pleasure," this term suggests a state where the person cannot experience normal pleasures most take for granted. In psychology, this condition could be due to depression or actual physical damage to the brain. Anhedonia can also be an unwanted side effect of some therapeutic drugs.

In addiction, anhedonia is a physical problem resulting from depletion of neural transmitters such as dopamine or serotonin and the so-called natural opiates, the endorphins (see Appendix B). Compounded by mental pain and depression, anhedonia can be relieved in a drug addict only by use of the drug. The condition can persist for as much as five years, during which time the addict seems lazy and apathetic.

The condition is real: the addict simply does not enjoy a sunrise, good meal, diverting movie, and so forth. Remaining completely free of mood-altering substances is a tough path to follow, but those who stay on the wagon (remain clean and sober) should feel some improvement in six months.

Cognitive Dissonance

The theory of cognitive dissonance (FEST57) says that people cannot hold conflicting views in their head for too long. The person will reject one or the other belief, or find some justification for merging the two, similar to Hegel's thesis and antithesis merging to form a synthesis.

Many studies have shown valid variations on the cognitive dissonance theme.   ARON63, for example, showed that students subjected to an embarrassing initiation reported more positive experiences in a neutral group than members who were admitted after a simple initiation. The members who had "suffered" most had to get the most out of the group to justify their suffering.

To resolve the conflict between the by-now obvious problems relating to their drug use and their denial of such consequences, an addict Stage 3 will frequently quit making excuses. The alcoholic gentleman no longer drinks because his wife nags. The mother no longer takes Valium because of her kids. The addict does not volunteer har formerly copious excuses and offers one only when required to deal with the law, parents, or the drug supplier.

Conversion Reaction

This condition has two varieties, which, again are probably part of a continuum. In what Freud termed hysteria, a person loses use of some part of their body. Se may be unable to move one arm, may be unable to speak, or unable to see. The numbness or paralysis makes no anatomical sense: the entire right hand is anesthetized while the right arm, enervated by the same plexus, shows no effects. Freud had fair success treating conversion reactions with hypnosis.

Also see psychosomatic illness.

Delusion

A delusion is an entire imaginary system. In a delusional state, the person believes se is being followed by the CIA for suspected spy activity. In its purest (worst) form, the delusion takes over: every phone number, license plate, and radio program fits in exactly with the plot.

Compare with "Hallucination." A hallucination seems more sensory, where a delusion involves the whole personality. (In spite of how it seems to the person experiencing the event, the hallucination may be completely generated in the brain, with no involvement of the sense organ.)

Double Blind

This is an experimental paradigm designed to minimize the influence of the experimenter on the subjects. Suppose we want to test the effects of Vitamin C in preventing colds. We make up Vitamin C tablets and put them in a bottle labeled XJ4528. We make up another batch of tablets, same size and color, with an acid taste, and put them into a bottle labeled RM8096. We randomly select a sufficient number of subjects to receive each tablet. We then give a nurse both bottles, telling har only which bottle is to be used for which person. In this type of study, the experimenter cannot by word or deed give a message like, "This will really make you feel better!"

(On an exam, a freshman psychology student at the University of Arkansas described double blind as "an experiment where noone knows what the hell is going on." He received full credit.)

Hallucination

"Seeing something that is not there" is a good definition of hallucinating, except that auditory hallucinations–hearing what is not there–are more common. A hallucination is the perception that some sensory event has occurred when there is no antecedent event to be sensed.

If a tree falls in the forest and there is no one there to hear it, does it make a sound? This seeming conundrum provides a way of understanding the hallucination. If we define sound as the wave moving through a medium such as air or the ground, the tree falling makes a sound. If we define sound as the movement of the huwan eardrum and resultant perceptions, the tree falling does not make a sound.

The hallucination is an artificial stimulation of some system in the perceptive pathway leading to an associative tract in the cortex and somehow (perhaps through microtubules in cells?) to consciousness. There is a real event in the sensory system, but it is not caused by the normal causative agent; it is an effect of a hallucinogenic substance.

Mescaline and LSD users have reported being able to see through solid objects such as a stop sign, table, or even an entire wall. The tripper is hallucinating in a peculair way: se is "seeing" what is behind the object, based on actual knowledge from a previous view or on a good guess.

Psychosomatic Illness

These illnesses are not "all in your head." The term comes from "somatic" relating to the body and "psycho" relating to the mind. Psychosomatic illness is an actual physical ailment that resulted from some ongoing mental stress. The classic case is the stomach ulcer that resulted from stress. (Although current evidence shows ulcers are an infection and can be treated with a powerful antibiotic, stress probably aggravates them.) The chronically depressed imagine a multitude of illnesses over a time. Gradually, this becomes a self-fulfilling prophecy, the immune system begins to break down, and the depressed person becomes really sick.

As with drug addiction, a psychosomatic illness cannot be treated with just psychotherapy. The stressful mental condition must be relieved and the medical condition must also be treated if any lasting results are to be obtained.

Reaction Formation

In this paradoxical condition, the person does the exact opposite of what se is really inclined to do. Someone who is very scared may act tough and threatening; someone who is very lonely may surround harself with constant companions. As explained previously, we all do this a little, but one who suffers from reaction formation feels the opposite of har facade and will go to extremes to prove the facade is real.

Self-Fulfilling Prophecy

Related to irony of fate in literature, the self-fulfilling prophecy is something that happens because we worry about it excessively or firmly believe it will happen. The athlete "psyching hamself up" to win a race or hit a home run is a good example of this. Another is someone who worries so much about Friday the Thirteenth that se cannot concentrate on driving. Se scrapes the side of a parked car and blames it on the unlucky day.

There is a dangerous side to this phenomenon. In one experiment (UNKN99), researchers told teachers they would administer IQ tests to first graders. When students completed the tests, researchers collected and secretly discarded the tests without looking at the results. Using suitable care to meet the standard bell curve, the researchers randomly assigned IQs to the children. With much pomp and ceremony, the researchers told the teachers which students were highly intelligent and which were stupid. Testing the children years later, the researchers found the students had a .8 (almost complete) correlation with the randomly-assigned scores.

For our purposes, this scary experiment is very important. If a parent constantly tells a child, "You're no good! You're lazy! You'll never amount to anything!" there is a good chance the child will grow up to fulfill that prophecy. Is our society really doing people a favor branding them a minority, giving them welfare payments for generations, and telling them they are "disadvantaged"? Or is society simply increasing the probability of addiction and other problems?

Appendix E
Gaynor Conventions

The English language is inherently biased because it uses masculine pronouns to refer to all people. (Other romance and Germanic languages are similarly biased, perhaps due to the influence of the Catholic Church during the Middle Ages.) We believe several thousand years is long enough for this stupid convention to enjoy such widespread usage.

The following new pronouns are proposed as substitutes for the exclusively-masculine terms currently in use.

Definition	New Term	Replaces
Reference to all people	wan	man, woman
	wankind	mankind
	wen	men, women
First person, singular	se	he, she
Third person	har	her, him
Third person, possessive	hars	hers, his

Please adopt the new terms in all writing. (Speech will be harder to change, because a person might be embarrassed to use the terms even if se feels they are proper.) You will find the substitutions have little effect on the flow of the passage. The new terms simply remove the masculine bias.

Also, please try to eliminate other racist and sexist language. American Negro males, for example, use "brother" to refer to another of their race and to exclude Caucasians. Feminists use "sister" for females of similar political persuasion. These terms are inaccurate because the person referred to is usually not the brother or sister of the speaker. The terminology merely supports racism or sexism.

Besides adding the new terms to your vocabulary, please use them in combining forms such as chairwan and policewan and stick to the concept by inventing other neutral terms as needed. Do not allow our very language to exclude slightly over half of our people.

Copyright holder grants permission to copy and distribute this sheet.[22]
Please pass this on to two others, especially congresswen.

© Gaynor Group, 1978

---

[22] Permission to distribute applies only to the Gaynor Conventions, which were originally on a single sheet of paper. Only the two-page Appendix where this footnote occurs may be freely distributed.

Afterword

In my experience, in the medical literature I have surveyed, and in the minds of those with whom I have spoken, there is no simple cure for drug addiction.   Recovery lies in a slow, methodical lessening of the probability of addiction.   Fighting drug addiction in society means appropriate treatment for the addicted and a continued battle against availability of the addicting substances.   When use of the drug stops, ancillary activities such as theft frequently stop also.

I wish there were a simple answer (a pill, perhaps) for all who suffer from addiction.   But, then, searching for a "quick fix" is part of the addict's problem!   A prayer alcoholics have passed around for years goes "Oh, God, please grant me patience, and RIGHT NOW!"   Quick, easy solutions are frequently addicting.

The suicide rate in the United States is approximately 1 in 8,000 (WEIT92)[23].   For cancer patients and other terminally ill people, it is greater than one in one hundred, an enormous increase: there is, of course, the certainty of lingering death.   For drug addicts, the suicide rate is one in four.   Add in overdoses (the unintentional ones), impure drugs, AIDS, and drug-related violence, and the chances of a Stage 3

---

[23] Some of mathematics here is mine. Source divides suicide according to several different categories: students, male vs. female, occupations. You will probably get different values with other sources. Also, some researchers (HIRS88) believe the number of suicides may be under reported by a factor of ten. Consider, for example, deliberate automobile accidents and strong religious prohibitions against suicide.

addict remaining alive are not good.

To fairly cover drug addiction, I must again emphasize several political points. Consider the license to kill that society has given legal drug pushers: tobacco and liquor companies. Nicotine products are addicting and dangerous, especially as cigarettes, which provide nicotine that can be smoked and inhaled. These products have no valid use and should not even be manufactured. While the statistics are careful not to say the drivers are actually drunk (a subjective term anyway), alcohol is allegedly "involved" in 50 to 70 percent of traffic accidents.

The contradiction of allowing some drugs and not others is used by the addict to justify the use of har drug of choice. Parental tirades to the contrary, it is a valid argument.

From the time our species came into being, it took about 25,000 years for the world's huwan population to double. Now it takes about seven and one half years. If we do not stop this absurd procreation, pollution, emerging viruses, or even mass insanity may take care of all our problems, including drug addiction. It is hypocritical to convince a recovering addict there is hope in a world where there is so little. Until we address problems of overcrowding, schools literally crumbling apart, barely inhabitable living quarters, and a military that spends enough each week to fix an entire city, it is going to be very difficult to convince addicts not to jump right back into the pipe accompanied by some crack or ice.

Halting drug addiction for more than 28 days (the typical time in treatment) means jobs for those trying to recover, an end to the "something for nothing" welfare mentality of the inner-city, an ecological environment where the air and water are not more danger-ous than many drugs, and a chance for all people to see some real hope. As far as drug addiction is a symptom of a personal problem, it is also a symptom of a problem with society as a whole.

The chances for recovery from drug addiction are not good, but I do not want to leave the impression such recovery is impossible. If one person has ever remained drug free for a substantial time, we know it is possible. Although the probability is not good, thousands (including me) have recovered.

David A. Peters
St. Paul, Minnesota
September 1996

Acknowledgements

I have avoided personal tragedies in this book. There are so many relating to drugs, and I did not want to write an encyclopedia. I want to mention a few, particularly close to me. Cathy, once a fund-raising supervisor for an orchestra, contracted AIDS sharing needles while shooting cocaine. Years ago, I rubbed calamine lotion on a prickly rash on her back. The skin, drawn drum-tight over her ribs, reminded me of concentration camp victims I had seen in WWII pictures.

After years of heavy amphetamine use, Wolf wanted to commit suicide. He filled the bathroom with natural gas from a small wall stove that did not have a pilot light. Deciding he wanted to be high when he died, he struck a match to light a joint. The explosion blew his house to pieces. He died hours later from the burns.

Jeanne was a tall, beautiful 20-year old with fuzzy red hair and the high cheek bones of a model. She used amphetamines, LSD, and alcohol for twenty years. When I last saw her, she had unsuccessfully covered up many sores on her skin with cheap makeup. I gently patted her abdomen which seemed to be carrying an eight-month old fetus. In answer to my query about its welfare, she replied, "Oh, I'm not pregnant. That's just my liver."

There are no parades or 21-gun salute when a drug addict dies. The President or mayor makes no speeches. When a teenager is shot, gun control fanatics use it for all sorts of press. Had this same teenager died in a basement with a plastic bag over har head, there would not even be a notice in the newspaper. It might embarrass the parents.

Stage 3 drug addicts are loners. They die in alleys with a needles hanging from their arms. Or tired of the needles, they jump from buildings into the alleys. Usually, there is not even an investigation. The reason is *not* because the cause of death is obvious. The cause of death is obvious when a presidential aide is found holding a gun whose caliber matches the hole in his head, yet the FBI spends several million investigating the aide's death. The death of drug addicts is not investigated simply because the event is so common.

I did not dedicate this book to those who have died of drug addiction because the group is not even well defined. Many addicts die from drug-induced suicides, AIDS, auto accidents in which a driver used some relatively untraceable drug (or no one bothered to check), cirrhosis which progresses after drug use stops, and so on, ad nauseam. Even deaths we are certain are due to drug use are too numerous to estimate, much less count or list. To prevent the many addicts from dying with no remembrance whatsoever, I mention them here. To thank even their memory seems morbid, so as Dylan once sung, "I'll just say fair thee well." Some would have become our doctors, fire-fighters, presidential aides, and perhaps even Nobel Prize winners.

For technical assistance, I thank

- Fred Bruno for writing the Foreword and for his patience with the money I owe him!
- Bob Burdick for editing suggestions in the Introduction;
- Dr. Earl McDowell who accepted the appendices for course work, allowing me to write while I attended grad school;
- Dr. Robert West for suggestions that this book include a separate chapter on social and legal implications of the probability theory. Without application, even the best theory (which I am not claiming!) remains just that.

I thank my father and mother for never abandoning me, whatever trouble I was in that year. My father died in the spring of 1994, having seen me drug free for only the last four years of my 30-year adult life.

Finally, I thank Aida Picardal, a rare individual (at least in my world) who has never used any addicting substance except coffee. Aida attends law school, fixes me breakfast, and occasionally listens to my problems with the manuscript and with life in general. She is not as patient as I would like, but a lot more patient than I would have been. For me, and perhaps for others, Aida has lowered The Probability of Addiction.

Bibliography

Much writing about addiction deals with personal tragedies, cultist methods of treatment (for or against), or self-help systems. I have avoided citing such work. Most sources cited here are scientific (empirical) studies or general information sources. I have listed a few, such as the classic ALCO39, which present an anecdotal view of addiction. BURR59, although classified as fictional, provides a memorable account of the street life of an addict.

References are indexed by the first four letters of the author's last name followed (with no space) by the year of publication. Occasionally, the four letters come from the title of familiar works such as *The Merck Index*. Modifications are made as needed for three-letter last names, unknown authors, dates not given. This bibliography generally conforms to American Psychological Association (APA) standards for citing reference works.

Although most sources support (or refute) some point in the book, some are listed because they supply additional information. MORG88, for instance, is a good book for a layperson or professional interested in drug effects. Although LUDW88 focuses on P_m, which I believe is not a major factor in addiction, it is well researched, and worthy of serious consideration. SHAF81 is an excellent source for information from all areas – medical, sociological, and personal – giving papers, abstracts, and many further references.

ALCO39   Alcoholics Anonymous. (1976). AA World Services, Inc., Third Edition, New York, New York. First published: 1939.

AMER75   American Medical Association. Quoted in Living Sober. (1975). Alcoholics Anonymous World Services, Inc. New York. Title page.

ARON59   Aronson, E. & Mills, J. (1959). The effect of the severity of initiation on liking for a group. Journal of Abnormal Social Psychology, vol. 59, p. 177-181.

BECK67   Becker, H. S. (1967). History, culture, and subjective experience: an exploration of the social bases of drug-induced experiences. Journal of Health and Social Behavior, 8, pp. 163-176.

BLIM90   Gene may be tied to 'virulent' alcoholism. (1990, 18 April). Science News, 137, 16, p. 246. Original work: Blum, K., Journal of the American Medical Association.

BOWE91   Bower, B. (1991, 21 September). Gene in the bottle. Science News, 140, 12, pp. 190-191.

BUCK73   Buckley, William F. (1973, January 1). Nixon and Kissinger: Triumph and Trial. Time. (First use I can find of term. Mr. Buckley did not apply it to all controlled substances.)

BURR59   Burroughs, W. (1959). Naked Lunch, Ballantine Books, Random House, Inc., New York, NY 10022.

EYSE81   Eysenck, H. J. & Kamin, L. (1981). The Intelligence Controversy. New York, Wiley, p. 97, passim.

FACK93   Fackelmann, K. A. (1993, February). Marijuana and

the brain. Science News, vol 143, p. 88-94. Original
research by Devane, W. A., National Institute of
Mental Health, Bethesda, Md.

FEST57   Festinger, L. (1957). A Theory of Cognitive Disso-
            nance, Harper & Row, New York.

GILB76   Gilbert, R. M. (1976). Caffeine as a drug of abuse.
            Research Advances in Alcohol and Drug Problems,
            vol. 3, p. 359-399.

GEND70   Gendreau, P. & Gendreau, L.P. (1970). The
            'addiction-prone' personality: a study of Canadian
            heroin addicts. Canadian Journal of Behavioral
            Science, vol. 2, p. 18-25.

GOLD71   Goldstein, A. (1971). Proceedings of the National
            Academy of Sciences, USA, Vol. 68, p. 1742.

HANC76   Hancock, John. (1776). The Declaration of Inde-
            pendence. The unanamous declaration of the
            Thirteen United States of America.

HIRS88   Hirshfield, R. M. A. and Goodwin, F. K. (1988). Risk
            Factors for Suicide. Review of Psychiatry. American
            Psychiatric Press. Washington D. C. Vol. 7.

HOLL91   Halloway, M. (1991, March). Rx for Addiction.
            Scientific American, Vol. 264, No. 2.

HORG93   Horgan, J. (1993, June). Eugenics revisited. Scien-
            tific American, pp. 122-131.

JENS69   Jensen, A. R. (1969). How can we boost IQ and
            scholastic achievement? Harvard Educational
            Review, 39, pp. 1-23.

JOHA76   Johanson, C.E., Balster, R.L., & Bonese, K. (1976).
          Self-administration of psychomotor stimulant drugs:
          the effects of unlimited access. Pharmacology and
          Biochemistry of Behavior, 4, pp. 45-51.

JONE84   Jones, R. T. (1984). The pharmacology of cocaine.
          Research 50 Monograph Series. Cocaine: Pharma-
          cology, Effects, and Treatment of Abuse, U.S. Gov-
          ernment Printing Office, Washington, D.C. 20402, p.
          34. (Entire article recommended.)

KAGA69   Kagan, J. (1969). Inadequate evidence and illogical
          conclusions. Harvard Educational Review, 39, pp.
          274-277.

LEND82   Lender, M. E. & Martin, J. K. (1982).   Drinking in
          America, The Free Press, Macmillan Publishing Co.,
          Inc., New York, NY, pp. 21-23.

LEWO76   Lewontin, R. C. (1976). Race and intelligence. The
          IQ controversy: critical readings. Block, N. J. &
          Dworkin, G. (Eds.), Pantheon, New York.

LITM76   Litman, G. K. (1976). Behavioral modification
          techniques in the treatment of alcoholism. Research
          Advances in Alcohol and Drug Problems, Plenum
          Press, New York.4, pp. 453-4.

LUDW88   Ludwig, A. M. (1988). Understanding the Alcoholic's
          Mind: The Nature of Craving and How to Control It.
          Oxford University Press, Inc., New York, NY 10016.

MACK84   Mackenzie, B. (1984). Explaining race differences
          in IQ: the logic, the methodology, and the evidence.
          American Psychologist, 39, 11, p. 1214-1233.

MASL54   Maslow, A. H. (1954). Motivation and Personality.
          Harper and Row, New York, New York.

MERC89   Budavari, S. (Ed.). (1989). The Merck Index,
          Eleventh Edition, Merck & Co., Inc., Rawhay, New
          Jersey.

MOOR89   Substance abuse among the disabled. (1989).
          Science News, 136, 15, p. 239. Original work:
          Moore, D. & Siegal, H. Alcohol Health and Research
          World, 13, 2.

MORG88   Morgan, R. (1988). The Emotional Pharmacy: How
          Mood-Altering & Psychoactive Drugs Work. The
          Body Press, Price Stern Sloan, Inc., Los Angles, CA
          90048.

MUEL88   Blood test linked to alcoholism risk. (1988, 21
          December). Science News, 135, 1, p. 13. Original
          work: Mueller, G. C, et. al., Proceedings of the
          National Academy of Sciences.

NAWS87   Narcotics Anonymous, Fourth Edition, World Service
          Office, Inc., Van Nuys, CA 91409, USA.

PAPO87   Papolos, D. F., M.D. & Papolos, J. (1987). Overcom-
          ing Depression. Harper & Row, Publishers, New
          York. Statement of Cavett, Dick, p. 8.

PART90   Ad campaign. (1990 and later). [television] Partner-
          ship for a Drug-Free America.

PDNE87   Hope and Recovery: A Twelve Step Guide for healing
          from compulsive sexual behavior. (1987). P.D.N.E.C,
          CompCare Publishers, Minneapolis, MN.

PERT73   Pert, C. B. & Snyder, S. H. (1973). Science, 179, p.
          1011.

PHYS91   Barnhart, E. R. (Pub.). (1991, or later). Physician's
          Desk Reference. Medical Economics Company, Inc.,

Oradell, N.J.

POLI79   Data from police officer regarding analysis of sub-
           stance seized in raid. (1979). (Numerous other
           sources cite low purity of street drugs.)

PSYC60   Hitchcock, A. (Director). & Bloch, R. (Writer).
           (1960). Psycho. [videotape] Shamley Productions,
           Inc.

RAWM78   Raw, M. (1978). The treatment of cigarette depen-
           dence. Research Advances in Alcohol and Drug
           Problems, Plenum Press, New York, 4, pp. 453-4.

RUBI89   Weakness for alcohol borne by muscles. (1989, 16
           February). Science News, 135, 8, p. 117. Original
           work: Rubin, E., et. al., New England Journal of
           Medicine.

SCIE88   Alcoholism's elusive genes. (1988). Science News,
           134, 5, pp. 74-75 ,79.

SELZ89   Selzer, M. L. (Date uncertain.) Michigan Alcoholism
           Screening Test.

SIMO73   Simon, E. J., et. al. (1973). Proceedings of the
           National Academy of Sciences. USA, 70, pg. 1947.

SHAF81   Shaffer, H. & Burglass, M. E. (1981). Classic Contri-
           butions in the Addictions. Department of Psychiatry,
           Harvard Medical School, Brunner/Mazel, Inc., 19
           Union Square, New York, NY.

SUND70   Sundance, R. (1970). <u>Not guilty on skid row.</u>
          <u>Recoveries: True Stories by People Who Conquered</u>
          <u>Addictions and Compulsions</u>. Hall, L. & Leigh, C.
          (Eds.). Cohn, Gurze Books, Carlsbad, CA 92008.

VOLK90   Probing cocaine in the heart and brain. (1990,
          June). <u>Science News</u>, 137, 26, p. 406. Original
          work: Volkow, N. D. <u>American Journal of Psychiatry</u>.

WEIT92   Weiten, Wayne. (1992). Psychology: Themes and
          Variations. Brooks/Cole Publishing Company division
          of Wadsworth, Inc. Pacific Grove, CA. p. 537,
          passim.

Index